THE CHRYSOSTOM BIBLE
A Commentary Series for Preaching and Teaching
Jeremiah: A Commentary

THE CHRYSOSTOM BIBLE
A Commentary Series for Preaching and Teaching

Jeremiah: A Commentary

Paul Nadim Tarazi

OCABS PRESS
ST PAUL, MINNESOTA 55124
2013

THE CHRYSOSTOM BIBLE
JEREMIAH: A COMMENTARY

Copyright © 2013 by
Paul Nadim Tarazi

ISBN 1-60191-024-X

All rights reserved.

PRINTED IN THE UNITED STATES OF AMERICA

Other Books by the Author

I Thessalonians: A Commentary

Galatians: A Commentary

The Old Testament: An Introduction

Volume 1: Historical Traditions, revised edition

Volume 2: Prophetic Traditions

Volume 3: Psalms and Wisdom

The New Testament: An Introduction

Volume 1: Paul and Mark

Volume 2: Luke and Acts

Volume 3: Johannine Writings

Volume 4: Matthew and the Canon

The Chrysostom Bible

Genesis: A Commentary

Philippians: A Commentary

Romans: A Commentary

Colossians & Philemon: A Commentary

1 Corinthians: A Commentary

Ezekiel: A Commentary

Joshua: A Commentary

2 Corinthians: A Commentary

Isaiah: A Commentary

Land and Covenant

The Chrysostom Bible
Jeremiah: A Commentary

Copyright © 2013 by Paul Nadim Tarazi
All rights reserved.

ISBN 1-60191-024-X

Published by OCABS Press, St. Paul, Minnesota.
Printed in the United States of America.

Books are available through OCABS Press at special discounts for bulk purchases in the United States by academic institutions, churches, and other organizations. For more information please email OCABS Press at press@ocabs.org.

Abbreviations

Books by the Author

1 Thess	*1 Thessalonians: A Commentary*, Crestwood, NY: St. Vladimir's Seminary Press, 1982
Gal	*Galatians: A Commentary*, Crestwood, NY: St. Vladimir's Seminary Press, 1994
OTI_1	*The Old Testament: An Introduction, Volume 1: Historical Traditions*, revised edition, Crestwood, NY: St. Vladimir's Seminary Press, 2003
OTI_2	*The Old Testament: An Introduction, Volume 2: Prophetic Traditions*, Crestwood, NY: St. Vladimir's Seminary Press, 1994
OTI_3	*The Old Testament: An Introduction, Volume 3: Psalms and Wisdom*, Crestwood, NY: St. Vladimir's Seminary Press, 1996
NTI_1	*The New Testament: An Introduction, Volume 1: Paul and Mark*, Crestwood, NY: St. Vladimir's Seminary Press, 1999
NTI_2	*The New Testament: An Introduction, Volume 2: Luke and Acts*, Crestwood, NY: St. Vladimir's Seminary Press, 2001
NTI_3	*The New Testament: An Introduction, Volume 3: Johannine Writings*, Crestwood, NY: St. Vladimir's Seminary Press, 2004
NTI_4	*The New Testament: An Introduction, Volume 4: Matthew and the Canon*, St. Paul, MN: OCABS Press, 2009
C-Gen	*Genesis: A Commentary*. The Chrysostom Bible. St. Paul, MN: OCABS Press, 2009
C-Phil	*Philippians: A Commentary*. The Chrysostom Bible. St. Paul, MN: OCABS Press, 2009
C-Rom	*Romans: A Commentary*. The Chrysostom Bible. St. Paul, MN: OCABS Press, 2010
C-Col	*Colossians & Philemon: A Commentary*. The Chrysostom Bible. St. Paul, MN: OCABS Press, 2010
C-1Cor	*1 Corinthians: A Commentary*. The Chrysostom Bible. St. Paul, MN: OCABS Press, 2011
C-Ezek	*Ezekiel: A Commentary*. The Chrysostom Bible. St. Paul, MN: OCABS Press, 2012

C-Josh   *Joshua: A Commentary.* The Chrysostom Bible. St. Paul, MN: OCABS Press, 2013

C-2Cor   *2 Corinthians: A Commentary.* The Chrysostom Bible. St. Paul, MN: OCABS Press, 2013

C-Is   *Isaiah: A Commentary.* The Chrysostom Bible. St. Paul, MN: OCABS Press, 2013

LAC   *Land and Covenant,* St. Paul, MN: OCABS Press, 2009

Abbreviations

Books of the Old Testament*

Gen	Genesis	Job	Job	Hab		Habakkuk
Ex	Exodus	Ps	Psalms	Zeph		Zephaniah
Lev	Leviticus	Prov	Proverbs	Hag		Haggai
Num	Numbers	Eccl	Ecclesiastes	Zech		Zechariah
Deut	Deuteronomy	Song	Song of Solomon	Mal		Malachi
Josh	Joshua	Is	Isaiah	Tob		Tobit
Judg	Judges	Jer	Jeremiah	Jdt		Judith
Ruth	Ruth	Lam	Lamentations	Wis		Wisdom
1 Sam	1 Samuel	Ezek	Ezekiel	Sir	Sirach	(Ecclesiasticus)
2 Sam	2 Samuel	Dan	Daniel	Bar		Baruch
1 Kg	1 Kings	Hos	Hosea	1 Esd		1 Esdras
2 Kg	2 Kings	Joel	Joel	2 Esd		2 Esdras
1 Chr	1 Chronicles	Am	Amos	1 Macc		1 Maccabees
2 Chr	2 Chronicles	Ob	Obadiah	2 Macc		2 Maccabees
Ezra	Ezra	Jon	Jonah	3 Macc		3 Maccabees
Neh	Nehemiah	Mic	Micah	4 Macc		4 Maccabees
Esth	Esther	Nah	Nahum			

Books of the New Testament

Mt	Matthew	Eph	Ephesians	Heb	Hebrews
Mk	Mark	Phil	Philippians	Jas	James
Lk	Luke	Col	Colossians	1 Pet	1 Peter
Jn	John	1 Thess	1 Thessalonians	2 Pet	2 Peter
Acts	Acts	2 Thess	2 Thessalonians	1 Jn	1 John
Rom	Romans	1 Tim	1 Timothy	2 Jn	2 John
1 Cor	1 Corinthians	2 Tim	2 Timothy	3 Jn	3 John
2 Cor	2 Corinthians	Titus	Titus	Jude	Jude
Gal	Galatians	Philem	Philemon	Rev	Revelation

*Following the larger canon known as the Septuagint.

Contents

Preface — 15
Introduction — 19

1 Introduction and Call of Jeremiah — 21
    Jeremiah's Call

2 The Sins of Jerusalem — 33
3 God Rejects His Chosen City — 39
4 The Covenant of the Lord — 57
    Instruction (musar) · Moses and Samuel · The Inclusion of the Nations on the Same Footing as Israel

5 Continued Disobedience to the Law — 79
6 The Wrath of God — 99
    The LXX compared to the MT

7 The Fate of the Exiles — 107
    Showdown between Jeremiah and the other prophets · Micah the Morashite · Bearing the Yoke · Confrontation with Hananiah · The Perennial Validity of Jeremiah's Message

8 The Book of Consolation — 129
    The Two Families · The Priority given to the Kingdom of the North · The Book of the Words of the Lord · The New Covenant · Looking ahead

9 The Demise of the City and the Rise of Scripture — 147
    The Sin of Zedekiah · The Rechabites (Rekabites) · Scripture, not Kingship and Temple, is the Legacy for the Future

10 Message over Messenger — 163
    Return to Egypt · The Queen of Heaven · The Book of Jeremiah canonizes itself as scripture

11 Oracles concerning the Nations — 173
Further Reading — 179

Preface

The present Bible Commentary Series is not so much in honor of John Chrysostom as it is to continue and promote his legacy as an interpreter of the biblical texts for preaching and teaching God's congregation, in order to prod its members to proceed on the way they started when they accepted God's calling. Chrysostom's virtual uniqueness is that he did not subscribe to any hermeneutic or methodology, since this would amount to introducing an extra-textual authority over the biblical texts. For him, scripture is its own interpreter. Listening to the texts time and again allowed him to realize that "call" and "read (aloud)" are not interconnected realities; rather, they are one reality since they both are renditions of the same Hebrew verb *qara'*. Given that words read aloud are words of instruction for one "to do them," the only valid reaction would be to hear, listen, obey, and abide by these words. All these connotations are subsumed in the same Hebrew verb *šama'*. On the other hand, these scriptural "words of life" are presented as readily understandable utterances of a father to his children (Isaiah 1:2-3). The recipients are never asked to engage in an intellectual debate with their divine instructor, or even among themselves, to fathom what he is saying. The Apostle to the Gentiles followed in the footsteps of the Prophets to Israel by handing down to them the Gospel, that is, the Law of God's Spirit through his Christ (Romans 8:2; Galatians 6:2) as fatherly instruction (1 Corinthians 4:15). He in turn wrote readily understandable letters to be read aloud. It is in these same footsteps that Chrysostom followed, having learned from both the Prophets and Paul that the same "words of life" carry also the sentence of death at the hand of the scriptural God, Judge of all

(Deuteronomy 28; Joshua 8:32-35; Psalm 82; Matthew 3:4-12; Romans 2:12-16; 1 Corinthians 10:1-11; Revelation 20:11-15).

While theological debates and hermeneutical theories come and go after having fed their proponents and their fans with passing human glory, the Golden Mouth's expository homilies, through the centuries, fed and still feed myriads of believers in so many traditions and countries. Virtually banned from dogmatic treatises, he survives in the hearts of "those who have ears to hear." His success is due to his commitment to exegesis rather than to futile hermeneutics. The latter behaves as someone who dictates on a living organism what it is supposed to be, whereas exegesis submits to that organism and endeavors to decipher it through trial and error. There is as much a far cry between the text and the theories about it as there is between a living organism and the theories about it. The biblical texts are the reality of God imparted through their being read aloud in the midst of the congregation, disregarding the value of the sermon that follows. The sermon, much less a theological treatise, is at best an invitation to hear and obey the text. Assessing the shape of an invitation card has no value whatsoever when it comes to the dinner itself; the guests are fed by the dinner, not by the invitation or its phrasing (Luke 14:16-24; Matthew 22:1-14).

This commentary series does not intend to promote Chrysostom's ideas as a public relation manager would do, but rather to follow in the footsteps of his approach as true children and heirs are expected to do. He used all the contemporary tools at his disposal to communicate God's written instruction to his hearers, as a doctor would with his patients, without spending unnecessary energy on peripheral debates requiring the use of professional jargon incomprehensible to the commoner. The writers of this series will try to do the same: muster to the best of their ability all necessary contemporary knowledge to communicate to the general readers the biblical message without burdening them with data unnecessary for that purpose. Whenever it will be deemed necessary or even helpful to do so, and in order to curtail burdensome and lengthy technical asides within the commentaries, specialized monographs related either to specific topics or to the scriptural background—literary, sociopolitical, or archeological—will be issued as companions to the series.

Paul Nadim Tarazi
Editor

Introduction

Position wise the Books of Jeremiah and Ezekiel stand at the center of the Hebrew Old Testament canon as well as at the center of the Latter Prophets. Both prophets were active around the time of the fall of Jerusalem to the Babylonians ca. 587 B.C., and their missions were to declare that the city succumbed to such a shameful end due to its negligence of God's law. What makes Jeremiah's message more ominous in the hearer's ears than that of Ezekiel is that he carried out his mission while living in Jerusalem. Ezekiel was already exiled in Babylonia when he delivered his message. While Ezekiel is the incontrovertible prophet of the Lord in his book, conversely in Jeremiah, other "prophets" named by name and endorsed by the majority of the people and leadership challenge Jeremiah at every step. Even an inattentive hearer can feel the "pain" of Jeremiah and thus tends to empathize with his frequent complaints. In this sense, the Book of Jeremiah stands alone in scripture as the book of God who implements his punishment in spite of any entreaty by the original addressees or by all subsequent generations of hearers down to the present. That is to say, it is the book where God "alone" stands "over the nations and over the kingdoms" of his entire earth (Jer 1:10) in his office of sole supreme judge of all, including the deities of the nations (Ps 82). This message of the Book of Jeremiah is, in a nutshell, precisely the basic teaching of the entire scripture of the Old Testament. I shall try to vindicate this assertion in my commentary by showing that, terminology wise, Jeremiah holds together that scripture in all its three parts—the Law, the Prophets, and the Writings—which in turn explains its intentional positioning by the biblical authors at the "heart" of the whole gamut of that literature. At "hearing" the Book of Jeremiah one is "hearing" the echo of the entire content of Old Testament literature after as well as before it. The Book of Ezekiel, the counterpart of Jeremiah, forms the other side of the diptych, and its function is to confirm that this perception is not merely an impression but reflects the fact of the matter.

Chapter 1
Introduction and Call of Jeremiah

The words of Jeremiah, the son of Hilkiah, of the priests who were in Anathoth in the land of Benjamin, to whom the word of the Lord came in the days of Josiah the son of Amon, king of Judah, in the thirteenth year of his reign. It came also in the days of Jehoiakim the son of Josiah, king of Judah, and until the end of the eleventh year of Zedekiah, the son of Josiah, king of Judah, until the captivity of Jerusalem in the fifth month. (Jer 1:1-3)

The introductory chapter of Jeremiah, like that of Isaiah and Ezekiel, contains in a nutshell the entire message of the book. In the face of the disobedience of all the people, the leaders and individuals alike, God chooses one person through whom he will relay his message—first of punishment and then of restoration. It is immaterial whether or not this person abides by the content of the message. Only the message is important. The worthiness of the chosen messenger, or lack thereof, is irrelevant. In the case of Jeremiah, this reality is underscored since he not only resists his calling as a prophet (v.6), but undergoes one crisis after another concerning his mission, and ends up in Egypt (43:4-6) even though he strictly forbade his co-Judeans to go there (42:1-43:3). In spite of everything, Jeremiah has no choice but to deliver the message. His career was chosen for him without any input on his part and regardless of his reticence and excuses:

Now the word of the Lord came to me saying, "Before I formed you in the womb I knew you, and before you were born I consecrated you; I appointed you a prophet to the nations." Then

> I said, "Ah, Lord God! Behold, I do not know how to speak, for I am only a youth." But the Lord said to me, "Do not say, 'I am only a youth'; for to all to whom I send you you shall go, and whatever I command you you shall speak. Be not afraid of them, for I am with you to deliver you, says the Lord." Then the Lord put forth his hand and touched my mouth; and the Lord said to me, "Behold, I have put my words in your mouth. See, I have set you this day over nations and over kingdoms, to pluck up and to break down, to destroy and to overthrow, to build and to plant." (1:4-10)

The superscription of the book reflects this reality. What the people hear are "the words of Jeremiah." He alone is privy to the fact that his words are under the direct dictate of God whose word (v.2) is communicated to Jeremiah through the medium of words (v.9b). As in most languages, the singular "word" is simply a literary expression referring to the entirety of a message that is always made up of "words." Unfortunately, under the undue influence of Platonic philosophy in the formulation of Patristic thought, the singular "word" came to mean an eternal reality standing on its own and existing per se independently from the "words." One should desist once and for all from injecting this understanding into the original scriptural text. In scripture not only is the "word" of God embedded in the words of scripture, but that "word," that is, message actually *comes out of* the scriptural "words" and thus does not exist *outside* let alone *before* the scriptural text. By the same token, one should desist from appealing to "inspiration," which is evocative of Plato's thesis of knowledge being merely a reminiscence of what the human soul

Introduction and Call of Jeremiah 23

knew already in its eternal existence.¹ Had Jeremiah been inspired in that sense, one commissioning would have been enough. He would not have needed the "word of the Lord" to come to him, at least, on two different occasions:² "The words of Jeremiah, the son of Hilkiah, of the priests who were in Anathoth in the land of Benjamin, to whom *the word of the Lord came in the days of Josiah* the son of Amon, king of Judah, in the thirteenth year of his reign. *It came also in the days of Jehoiakim* the son of Josiah, king of Judah, and until the end of the eleventh year of Zedekiah, the son of Josiah, king of Judah, until the captivity of Jerusalem in the fifth month." (vv.1-3) The phraseology of this superscription corresponds to the structure of the book itself: Jeremiah's mission under Josiah is covered in chapters 1-20, whereas his activity under Jehoiakim starts with chapter 21. Thus, Jeremiah never "became" a prophet as though he changed professions, pursued a new career, or held a new office. He remained throughout his life "Jeremiah, the son of Hilkiah, of the priests who were in Anathoth in the land of Benjamin" (1:1) who had been commissioned expressly to "prophesy," just like his predecessor Amos:

> And Amaziah [the priest of Bethel] said to Amos, "O seer, go, flee away to the land of Judah, and eat bread there, and prophesy there; but never again prophesy at Bethel, for it is the king's sanctuary, and it is a temple of the kingdom." Then Amos answered Amaziah, "I am no prophet, nor a prophet's son; but I am a herdsman, and a dresser of sycamore trees, and the Lord took

---

¹ My readers are reminded that in Plato the souls are of the same "texture" as God: an eternally pre-existent "idea" or "form."
² Actually one hears time and again that "the word of the Lord came" to Jeremiah (1:4, 11, 13; 2:1; 11:1; 13:3, 8; 16:1; 18:5; 24:4; 28:12; 32:6; 33:1, 19, 23; 34:12; 36:27; 39:15; 49:34).

me from following the flock, and the Lord said to me, 'Go, prophesy to my people Israel.'" (7:12-15)

This is confirmed by another feature of the superscription in Jeremiah, unique to the prophetic books, where reference is made to both the "words of the prophet" (v.1) and the "word of the Lord" (v.2). It even emphasizes the former by relegating the Lord to a relative clause ("The words of Jeremiah ... to whom the word of the Lord came ..."). It also reflects the unique situation of Jeremiah in that he spoke at such varied times and settings: under Josiah (627-609), under Jehoiakim (609-597), during the first deportation to Babylon (597),[3] under Zedekiah (597-587), during the sack of Jerusalem (587), and briefly in Egypt. Given the multiplicity of occasions when Jeremiah prophesied, the plural "words of Jeremiah" naturally seem to warrant more emphasis than the singular "word of God." This understanding finds support in Amos, the only other prophetic book that describes its contents as the words of its namesake rather than as the word of God (1:1). There we hear the prophet addressing three different "words" on three different occasions: "Hear this word that the Lord has spoken against you, O people of Israel, against the whole family which I brought up out of the land of Egypt" (3:1); "Hear this word, you cows of Bashan, who are in the mountain of Samaria, who oppress the poor, who crush the needy, who say to their husbands, 'Bring, that we may drink!'" (4:1); "Hear this word which I take up over you in lamentation, O house of Israel." (5:1)

---

[3] Included in the period between Jehoiakim and Zedekiah; see 2 Kg 24:6-17.

Introduction and Call of Jeremiah

The text in Jeremiah reflects the understanding, at least on the part of its writers, that in order to function as God's special emissary Jeremiah had to be commissioned anew each time the necessity arose. The assertion that he was chosen from his mother's womb and consecrated to this kind of life before his birth (1:5) in no way contradicts this conclusion, since the intention of that statement is simply to underscore the fact that Jeremiah had no choice in the matter.[4]

Jeremiah's Call

In Isaiah's call narrative (ch.6) it is the *glory* of the Lord that forms the background of Isaiah's activity. In the call of Jeremiah (ch.1) the *word* of the Lord takes center stage right from the beginning. It is this word that governs Jeremiah's life[5] and begins its work, even before his birth when God pronounced his consecration as a prophet "to the nations" (v.5). This last phrase may seem inappropriate since his mission is actually to Judah, his own country, even if it includes pronouncing oracles against the nations.[6] The reason for such phraseology is that Jeremiah prophesied during the fall of Jerusalem and the concomitant collapse of Judah as an independent socio-political entity. Thus this Judahite priest from Anathoth became a man without a country and so became a witness for his God to the entire Near East. Direct evidence for the "universal" perspective to his prophecy may be found in his second vision: the background for

---

[4] See below.
[5] Notice the repetition of the expression "the word of the Lord came to me" in vv.4, 11 and 13. Notice also its use in 2:1 where it is followed by Jeremiah's opening statement, "Hear the word of the Lord" (2:4).
[6] Jer 25:14-38; 46-51. Notice the similar situation in Am 1-2.

the word the Lord is about to fulfill (v.12) is none other than the siege of Jerusalem (v.15) *as part of* the Babylonian sweep over the entire ancient Near East (vv.14-15).[7] In other words, from the beginning the nations are an integral part of Jeremiah's mission; actually, according to vv.13-16, it is the Babylonian siege that will set the stage for the implementation of the Lord's word against Jerusalem.[8]

Verse 5 explains that this wide-ranging mission of Jeremiah was assigned to him long before he could have any say in the matter. Such a statement is to be read in context, not as a proof text in a theological debate about issues totally foreign to it, such as free will and predestination. The verse's function is to preempt any attempt by Jeremiah to get himself out of the picture already drawn by God (v.6) when he is finally called upon to take his place in it (note the words "this day" in v.10). The point is that the matter was settled many years beforehand, and Jeremiah now has no say whatsoever in the matter: he shall go to wherever he is sent, he shall speak whatever he is commanded to say (v.7), and that is the end of that! The forestalling of any objections on his part makes sense because if he did have a choice he certainly would have opted out of this particular assignment. From the start it sounds unpleasant and downright dangerous: why else would he need to be reassured that the Lord would *deliver him* (v.8)? Jeremiah is like a soldier sent by his commanding officer to the front line of a raging battle; his will

---

[7] The nations conquered and subdued by their conquerors—in this case, the Babylonians—would be forced to join their alliance and thus behave as enemies toward the peoples that were next in line on the conqueror's route. See Jer 25:13b-38 on the Babylonian sweep over the ancient Near Eastern nations.

[8] See below.

Introduction and Call of Jeremiah

in the matter is of no account. He must simply go and do what he is commanded to do.

The task assigned to him is to deliver a message. To emphasize again that his own desires are irrelevant, he is informed that he will not even get to choose his own words. The same hand that formed him in the womb and consecrated him to be a prophet will pour God's words into his mouth (v.9). For the most part they will not be pleasant words. What makes Jeremiah's task a dangerous one is the fact that those words will be, first and foremost, harbingers of destruction and only secondarily will they be words of building up again (v.10).[9] Since he has no choice whatsoever, he is not given the chance to debate the matter with God, as Amos was able to do.[10] He is simply summoned to see what God wants him to see and report it faithfully.

The two commissioning visions are related.[11] The first, based on a play on words between *šaqed* (almond tree) and *šoqed* (watching over), informs Jeremiah that the Lord is watching over his word with the intent of "doing it," that is, of doing what he said he would do:

> And the word of the Lord came to me, saying, "Jeremiah, what do you see?" And I said, "I see a rod of almond." Then the Lord said to me, "You have seen well, for I am watching over my word to perform it." (vv. 11-12)

One notices again how Jeremiah's mission is under the aegis of the will of the Lord and controlled by it. It is as if his function is

---

[9] As is clear from the rest of ch.1.
[10] See comments on Am 7:1-6 in *OTI₂* 68-73.
[11] This was also the case with Amos; see Am 7:7-9; 8:1-3. In the latter case, the word play is between *qays* (summer fruit) and *qes* (end) in v.1.

merely to act as a channel for that will. The "word" that the Lord is watching over to realize to a T—including the final restoration after the punishment—is none other than the "words" he just put in Jeremiah's mouth: "Behold, I have put my words in your mouth. See, I have set you this day over nations and over kingdoms, to pluck up and to break down, to destroy and to overthrow, to build and to plant." (vv.9a-10) Such will be confirmed later in the book on God's lips no less: "And it shall come to pass that as I have watched over (*šaqadti*) them to pluck up and break down, to overthrow, destroy, and bring evil, so I will watch over (*'ešqod*) them to build and to plant, says the Lord." (31:28) It is worthwhile to point out that one finds here a perfect example of how scripture is the product of one school that orchestrated the entire gamut of writings. It cannot be happenstance that the latter verse reflects teachings concerning the exile found in both Ezekiel and Isaiah. The immediately following verses are, in fact, a compact version of Ezekiel 18:

> In those days they shall no longer say: "The fathers have eaten sour grapes, and the children's teeth are set on edge." But every one shall die for his own sin; each man who eats sour grapes, his teeth shall be set on edge. (Jer 31:29-30)

> What do you mean by repeating this proverb concerning the land of Israel, 'The fathers have eaten sour grapes, and the children's teeth are set on edge'? As I live, says the Lord God, this proverb shall no more be used by you in Israel. Behold, all souls are mine;

the soul of the father as well as the soul of the son is mine: the soul that sins shall die. (Ezek 18:2-4)[12]

On the other hand, the use of four verbs depicting divine punishment (to pluck up and to break down, to destroy and to overthrow; Jer 1:10 and 31:28)[13] compared to only two describing restoration (to build and to plant; 1:10; 31:28) is an echo of the announcement of the end of the exile in Isaiah: "Comfort, comfort my people, says your God. Speak tenderly to Jerusalem, and cry to her that her warfare is ended, that her iniquity is pardoned, that she has received from the Lord's hand *double for all her sins*." (40:1-2)

The second commissioning vision (Jer 1:13-19) reveals what the Lord is going to do:

> [13]The word of the Lord came to me a second time, saying, "What do you see?" And I said, I see a boiling pot, facing away from the north." [14]Then the Lord said to me, "Out of the north evil shall break forth upon all the inhabitants of the land. [15]For lo, I am calling all the tribes of the kingdoms of the north, says the Lord; and they shall come and every one shall set his throne at the entrance of the gates of Jerusalem, against all its walls around about, and against all the cities of Judah. [16]And I will utter my judgments against them, for all their wickedness in forsaking me; they have burned incense to other gods; and worshiped the works of their own hands. [17]But you, gird up your loins; arise, and say to them everything that I command you. Do not be dismayed by them, lest I dismay you before them. [18]And I, behold, I make you

---

[12] What follows is a lengthy passage (Ezek 18:5-32) filled with detailed examples backing the individual accountability for one's righteousness or lack thereof.

[13] In Jer 31:28 we hear the additional "to bring evil," which is an appositional explanation of the object of the divine fourfold action.

this day a fortified city, an iron pillar, and bronze walls, against the whole land, against the kings of Judah, its princes, its priests, and the people of the land. ¹⁹They will fight against you; but they shall not prevail against you, for I am with you, says the Lord, to deliver you."

The "boiling pot, facing away from the north" refers to the Babylonian push toward the Eastern Mediterranean (v.14). This is just the beginning; Babylon's siege of Jerusalem and Judah (v.15b) is not the ultimate purpose of God's plan; it merely sets the stage for the more important conflict between Judah and Jeremiah.[14] Nevertheless, the Lord's word here is not describing background circumstances, but is actively creating them—the besiegers of Jerusalem will come because the Lord has called them (v.15a). His purpose in calling them is to carry out punishment against Judah for its sins (v.16). It is this divine judgment against Judah that Jeremiah is to proclaim to his countrymen (v.17a). In repeating that message to them, Jeremiah is not to show any fear (v.17b);[15] if he does, then the Lord himself, not the Judahites, will give Jeremiah a good reason for it (v.17c)! Why does it matter whether Jeremiah shows fear or not? The reason is that God's city is no longer Jerusalem; "this day" Jeremiah himself has become God's city (v.18a) in order to implement the word just spoken on "this day" (v.16a). As a city is besieged, so shall Jeremiah be beset by Judahites (v.18b). They will fight against him (v.19a) because of his unwelcome message, yet they will not prevail. The Lord himself will deliver Jeremiah from them (v.19b).

---

[14] Described in vv.18-19; see below.
[15] Notice the parallelism between vv.7c-8a and v.17.

The siege of Jerusalem by the Babylonians is then the backdrop, the set on the stage, so to speak. What is *really* happening—that is, what really interests Jeremiah's God—is that the Lord himself is being fought against and besieged by "the kings of Judah, its princes, its priests, and the people of the land" (v.18b). The putative "people of the Lord" are in truth attacking him in his own stronghold and on his own throne, but "they shall not prevail" (v.19b). Indeed, they cannot, because suddenly he is no longer located in the Holy of Holies of the Jerusalem temple. Rather, he is ensconced in his new city, that is, in his prophet Jeremiah, and cannot possibly be overthrown, since the uttered word is beyond the reach of even those who might destroy its originator.

The words God formerly put in the mouths of his temple priests through the established *torah* are now communicated through Jeremiah's mouth. The difference between the two is that the *torah* is connected with a shrine, whereas the words of Jeremiah are independent of any locale and thus are indestructible. Those who do not want to hear his message can "debar Jeremiah from going to the house of the Lord," but he can circumvent that by telling Baruch to write down his words and go to the temple and proclaim them for him there (36:5-6). King Jehoiakim can even destroy the scroll written with Jeremiah's words (v.23), but again to no avail; upon the Lord's expressed order (vv.27-28), "Jeremiah took another scroll and gave it to Baruch ... who wrote on it, at the dictation of Jeremiah, *all* the words of the scroll which Jehoiakim king of Judah had burned in the fire"—and even "many similar words were added to them" (v.32). That scroll and other additions to it will grow into the book of Jeremiah and will be recognized as scripture wherein the Lord is encountered through his abiding word. And it will continue to abide long after those who wanted to silence Jeremiah are dead and the temple they trusted in is a pile of rubble.

Chapter 2
The Sins of Jerusalem

In the book of Isaiah, after the introductory chapter there are a few chapters (2-5) describing the sins of Jerusalem and Judah that warrant the intervention of God through his prophet.[1] In the book of Jeremiah, we encounter the same approach. Before the first official assignment at the entrance to the Temple of Jerusalem where Jeremiah will openly address "*all* you men of Judah who enter these gates to worship the Lord" (7:2b)—"the priests and the prophets and all the people" (26:7a)—chapters 2-6 cover in detail their sin that warranted God's intervention through another prophet. This structural parallelism is further evident in that both Isaiah 2-5 and Jeremiah 2-6 have at their center the promise of the new restored Zion (Is 4:2-5; Jer 3:14-18), which will include the nations (Is 2:2-4; Jer 3:17), in order to give hope to the hearers in the midst of an otherwise overwhelming indictment. The content of Jeremiah 2-6 is also reminiscent of the teaching of Ezekiel, Jeremiah's contemporary, concerning the sin of Jerusalem. Thus Jeremiah, literarily, forms a bridge between the two prophetic books that bracket it.[2]

In Isaiah the vocabulary of 4:2-5 describing the new Zion corresponds to that of the rest of the book.[3] Here also, in

---

[1] *C-Is* 59.
[2] This militates, as I showed time and again in my commentaries, for one school behind the production of the Latter Prophets.
[3] *C-Is* 61-62.

Jeremiah, the new Zion is described in a way that suits the message of Jeremiah:

> Return, O faithless children, says the Lord; for I am your master; I will take you, one from a city and two from a family, and I will bring you to Zion. And I will give you shepherds after my own heart, who will feed you with knowledge and understanding. Any when you have multiplied and increased in the land, in those days, says the Lord, they shall no more say, "The ark of the covenant of the Lord." It shall not come to mind, or be remembered, or missed; it shall not be made again. At that time Jerusalem shall be called the throne of the Lord, and all nations shall gather to it, to the presence of the Lord in Jerusalem, and they shall no more stubbornly follow their own evil heart. In those days the house of Judah shall join the house of Israel, and together they shall come from the land of the north to the land I gave your fathers for a heritage. (3:14-18)

The passage starts (v.14a) with an invitation to "return" (*šub*), a verb that is a staple of Jeremiah. Its use is further underscored through word play whereby the addressees are "faithless," literally meaning "those who turn away (apostates)" (*šobabim*, from the verb *šub*). Moreover "I am your master" (*ba'alti bakem*, v. 14b) looks ahead to the only other occurrence of the verb *ba'al* (be the master of) in a passage concerning the new covenant: "Behold, the days are coming, says the Lord, when I will make a new covenant with the house of Israel and the house of Judah, not like the covenant which I made with their fathers when I took them by the hand to bring them out of the land of Egypt, my covenant which they broke, though I was their husband (*ba'alti bam*), says the Lord." (31:31-32) These two instances are linked through the reference to "the house of Israel and the house of Judah" which we hear in both passages.

The closeness of Jeremiah to Ezekiel is also evident. Consider the following:

1. The repetitive stress on Jerusalem's harlotry with many nations and their gods as her lovers: Jeremiah 3:1-9; 5:7 and Ezekiel 16 (passim); 23 (passim); 43:7. Furthermore, harlotry is committed by both Israel and Judah (Jer 3:6-10), however, Judah is considered more guilty of such (v.11; see Ezek 16:46, 51-52; 23:11).

2. Jerusalem is referred to metaphorically as God's faithless wife (Jer 3:1, 8; 5:1) and daughter (4:11, 31; 6:2, 23, 26) just as in Ezekiel 16.

3. The two houses of Judah and Israel will be joined at the restoration (Jer 3:14; Ezek 37:15-28) and become one new people being led by shepherds instead of kings (Jer 3:15; Ezek 37:23-24).

4. The punishment is instructional and entails an invitation to repentance (Jer 3:11- 4:4; 6: 8-9; Ezek 11:14-21).

5. One of the purposes of the famine sent by God in the land of plenty (Jer 5:20-25; Ezek 5:16-17; 14:13, 21) is to remind the people that he is the dispenser of bread (Ezek 16:19), which he was able to provide even in the wilderness (Jer 2:1-7).

6. Ezekiel is assigned the function of "watchman" (*sopheh*) for God (3:17; 33:2-7), so also are the prophets, among whom is Jeremiah (6:17),

which is the only instance of that noun in Jeremiah.[4]

7. Just as in Ezekiel (2:3), the trait of disobedience goes back to the forefathers who were no better than Jeremiah's contemporaries: "Let us lie down in our shame, and let our dishonor cover us; for we have sinned against the Lord our God, we and our fathers, from our youth even to this day; and we have not obeyed the voice of the Lord our God." (Jer 3:25)

8. In Ezekiel, whenever the nations are used to carrying out the verdict of divine punishment, they are likened to God's assembly (*qahal*). The same is found in Jeremiah:

> They (your lovers, that is, the Babylonians) shall bring up a host (*qahal*) against you, and they shall stone you and cut you to pieces with their swords. (Ezek 16:40)

> And they shall come against you from the north with chariots and wagons and a host (*qahal*) of peoples; they shall set themselves against you on every side with buckler, shield, and helmet, and I will commit the judgment to them, and they shall judge you according to their judgments. (23:24)

> For thus says the Lord God: "Bring up a host (*qahal*) against them, and make them an object of terror and a spoil. And the host (*qahal*) shall stone them and dispatch them with their swords; they

---

[4] RSV's "watchmen" in Jer 31:6 and 51:12 are from two different Hebrew roots *noṣer* and *šomer*, respectively.

shall slay their sons and their daughters, and burn up their houses." (23:46-47)

> For behold, I am stirring up and bringing against Babylon a company (*qahal*) of great nations, from the north country; and they shall array themselves against her; from there she shall be taken. Their arrows are like a skilled warrior who does not return empty-handed. (Jer 50:9)

9. What is impressive in Jeremiah is that, in the case of the judgment against "this people" (6:19), that is, Judah, he appeals to the nations as *'edah* (congregation), which is a classical scriptural designation of God's official gathering of his people:[5]

> I set watchmen over you, saying, "Give heed to the sound of the trumpet!" But they said, "We will not give heed." Therefore hear, O nations, and know, O congregation (*'edah*), what will happen to them. Hear, O earth; behold, I am bringing evil upon this people, the fruit of their devices, because they have not given heed to my words; and as for my law, they have rejected it. (6:17-19)

10. Finally, later in the book, we shall learn that Jeremiah is among those of Judah who go to Egypt (43:7); Ezekiel is among the exiles he is preaching to (12:1-6).

---

[5] *qahal* is usually translated into *ekklēsia* (church in the New Testament) and *'edah* into *synagōgē* (synagogue in the New Testament) in the LXX.

Chapter 3
God Rejects His Chosen City

Now that the temple is bereft of the One who was its raison d'être, the *torah* connected with it is no longer the Lord's instruction but merely the temple priests' opinion. The Lord's teaching is to be found in Jeremiah, his new abode:

> The word that came to Jeremiah from the Lord: "Stand in the gate of the Lord's house, and proclaim there this word, and say, Hear the word of the Lord, all you men of Judah who enter these gates to worship the Lord. Thus says the Lord of hosts, the God of Israel, Amend your ways and your doings, and I will let you dwell in this place. Do not trust in these deceptive words: 'This is the temple of the Lord, the temple of the Lord, the temple of the Lord' … Behold you trust in deceptive words to no avail." (7:1-4, 8)

As of now, Jeremiah's word *is* the Lord's word. And this word solemnly warns all who blindly trust in the sanctity of the temple as a guarantee of protection that they are making a mistake. What the people should have done to ensure peace and safety for themselves was to implement God's will, namely, to "truly execute justice one with another" (v.5). Instead, they oppressed the alien, the fatherless and the widow, they shed innocent blood, and they went after other gods (v.6; see also v.9). And they did all this while shamelessly standing before the Lord in his house, thinking God either didn't see or didn't care and would deliver them from danger anyway (v.10). But Jeremiah drops a bombshell. God does see, and he does care, and because of the sins of his people he is prepared to do to Jerusalem what he once did to Shiloh:

Has this house, which is called by my name, become a den of robbers in your eyes? Behold I myself have seen it, says the Lord. Go now to my place that was in Shiloh, where I made my name dwell at first, and see what I did to it for the wickedness of my people Israel. And now, because you have done all these things, says the Lord, and when I spoke to you persistently you did not listen, and when I called you, you did not answer, therefore I will do to the house which is called by my name, and in which you trust, and to the place which I gave to you and to your fathers, as I did to Shiloh. (vv.11-14)

To understand the effect this message would have on its listeners, one must realize that, in scripture, by the end of the 7th century B.C. Jerusalem was viewed as *the* city God had ultimately chosen to be his.[1] Shiloh, on the other hand, was a shrine of the northern Kingdom of Israel, a kingdom that (in Judah's eyes) had illegally repudiated the Davidic dynasty and for its apostasy had suffered destruction and exile as divine punishment.[2] Shiloh itself had been destroyed long before that, and for the same kind of sin committed by its priests and people.[3] The Judahites of Jeremiah's day would have considered Shiloh to be synonymous with apostasy, the very epitome of evil according to the Law, especially that of Deuteronomy which championed the oneness of the valid place of worship.[4] Therefore, to put God's chosen city Jerusalem on par with idolatrous, disgraced Shiloh would have been blasphemous at best. After all, for the Jerusalemite priesthood, the Lord and God

---

[1] See Ps 78:67-69.
[2] See 2 Kg 18:11-12.
[3] See Ps 78:56-64; 1 Sam 2-3. The sins of Eli and his sons are also what occasioned God's raising up of Samuel, through whom he anointed David his chosen one (Ps 78:70-72).
[4] Deut 12:2-14; 14:22-25; 16:1-17; see also the debate between the tribes concerning this matter in Josh 22.

of Judah was *by definition* the God of Jerusalem! How could they stand idly by while Jeremiah not only flatly contradicted that official viewpoint,[5] but also in so doing suggested the inevitability of the destruction of their city? He must have sounded like a traitor to his country. The violent reaction to his message is no different from that received by people considered to be traitors in all ages before and since.

The negative aspect of Jeremiah's message evoked a nasty response. There was, however, also a positive aspect to his message. Jeremiah did not simply reject the official vantage point as false; he proclaimed a different perspective to be true. He asserted that the Lord's name was what mattered: God is not defined by or tied to any city but is free to make "his name" dwell wherever he chooses. His name had once dwelt in Shiloh, which he forsook; it once dwelled in Jerusalem but he forsook that city; it now dwells in his prophet Jeremiah.[6]

This is where Jeremiah diverges from the path set by the temple leaders. The Mosaic *torah*, as viewed by the priests, circumscribed God within the world of the temple and Jerusalem. Jeremiah's God was totally free of such limitations. Having abandoned this aspect of the official teaching, Jeremiah had no choice but to abandon another: he offered no hope for escape from God's judgment. The Deuteronomic promises of blessings for obedience and curses for disobedience always offered the people hope for the future—if they would just change their ways, God would be sure to transform hard times into good times. But after publicly

---

[5] Ps 78:56-72 constitutes a summary of this viewpoint.
[6] See earlier on ch.1; see also 7:12.

rejecting Jerusalem and adopting Jeremiah as his mouthpiece, the Lord could not allow Jerusalem to remain unharmed because that would have confirmed the validity of the perspective of those who believed he was tied to that city or defined by it. Its salvation would have proven Jeremiah wrong and his opponents right in the most basic issue that divided them. So Jeremiah was not even allowed to pray or intercede for the people already marked for perdition. If he were to try, God warned that he would not listen (v.16). His verdict of total annihilation was final (v.20; also vv.27-34): Judah and Jerusalem would join Israel and Samaria in their fate (v.34).

To further justify the promised destruction, the parenthetical passage (vv. 21-26) concerning the Law's prescriptions again emphasizes the incompatibility between priestly *torah* and Jeremiah's *dabar* (word). From the beginning God did not require sacrifices (the temple's chief function), but rather obedience to his voice, and his voice could always be heard from his "servants the prophets" (v. 25). However, if rejecting temple and *torah* paved the way for the destruction of Jerusalem, it also paved the way for post-destruction renewal. A God who was defined as the God of Jerusalem and was committed to doing everything in his power to protect it would have been a laughingstock at best after Jerusalem went up in smoke. But a God who had openly rejected that view of himself as false beforehand, and who had shown that he could make his abode wherever he pleased, would be able to take again an active role in the life of his people after the destruction of the city that had become filled with idols. And this is precisely the idea of the "new covenant" as witnessed to in Jeremiah 31:31-34.

This anti-temple stand is pushed to its most extreme in the phraseology of the end of the divine verdict:

> Therefore, behold, the days are coming, says the Lord, when it will no more be called Topheth, or the valley of the son of Hinnom, but the valley of Slaughter: for they will bury in Topheth, because there is no room elsewhere. And the dead bodies of this people will be food for the birds of the air, and for the beasts of the earth; and none will frighten them away. And I will make to cease from the cities of Judah and from the streets of Jerusalem the voice of mirth and the voice of gladness, the voice of the bridegroom and the voice of the bride; for the land shall become a waste. At that time, says the Lord, the bones of the kings of Judah, the bones of its princes, the bones of the priests, the bones of the prophets, and the bones of the inhabitants of Jerusalem shall be brought out of their tombs; and they shall be spread before the sun and the moon and all the host of heaven, which they have loved and served, which they have gone after, and which they have sought and worshiped; and they shall not be gathered or buried; they shall be as dung on the surface of the ground. (7:32-8:2)

These words bring to mind a similar verdict found in Ezekiel:

> While the man was standing beside me, I heard one speaking to me out of the temple; and he said to me, "Son of man, this is the place of my throne and the place of the soles of my feet, where I will dwell in the midst of the people of Israel for ever. And the house of Israel shall no more defile my holy name, neither they, nor their kings, by their harlotry, and by the dead bodies of their kings, by setting their threshold by my threshold and their doorposts beside my doorposts, with only a wall between me and them. They have defiled my holy name by their abominations which they have committed, so I have consumed them in my anger. Now let them put away their idolatry and the dead bodies of their kings far from me, and I will dwell in their midst for ever." (43:6-9)

In order to comprehend such aversion, even against the "bones" and "dead bodies" of monarchs, a digression is in order. The entire socio-polity of the Ancient Near East world was woven around the temple-palace complex of the capital or major city of a given society. The main representative of the city's deity was the monarch who, as the "son of the deity" (son of God; divine son; royal son; Ps 72:1), wielded absolute authority over the entire city and its two foci, the palace and the temple. He was de facto the high priest, as is clear from the fact that King Solomon was the one who, at the inauguration of the temple, both blessed the people (1 Kg 8:14) and prayed on and in behalf of them (vv.30-61) as well as for himself (vv.22-29). Since the administration of the palace and public life took most of his time, a monarch would appoint at will one of the priests as high priest (2:35b), who would be his locum tenens in the temple service. That is why whenever a city was overtaken, the conqueror would "decapitate" it by taking away its leadership consisting mainly of the residents and servers of the temple-palace complex, often leaving the general populace in place:

> And Nebuchadnezzar king of Babylon came to the city, while his servants were besieging it; and Jehoiachin the king of Judah gave himself up to the king of Babylon, himself, and his mother, and his servants, and his princes, and his palace officials. The king of Babylon took him prisoner in the eighth year of his reign, and carried off all the treasures of the house of the Lord, and the treasures of the king's house, and cut in pieces all the vessels of gold in the temple of the Lord, which Solomon king of Israel had made, as the Lord had foretold. He carried away all Jerusalem, and all the princes, and all the mighty men of valor, ten thousand captives, and all the craftsmen and the smiths; none remained, except the poorest people of the land. And he carried away

Jehoiachin to Babylon; the king's mother, the king's wives, his officials, and the chief men of the land, he took into captivity from Jerusalem to Babylon. And the king of Babylon brought captive to Babylon all the men of valor, seven thousand, and the craftsmen and the smiths, one thousand, all of them strong and fit for war. And the king of Babylon made Mattaniah, Jehoiachin's uncle, king in his stead, and changed his name to Zedekiah. (2 Kg 24:11-17)

Instead of accepting their human fate that the endurance of their throne through the ages (Ps 45:6a) is secured through their dynasty (vv.16-17a) rather than through their own person, kings decided, due to their hubris, to take the matter into their own hands and started building mausoleums—large stately tombs—to preserve their "dead bodies" *forever*. The most extreme examples of such endeavors are the pyramids and the tombs of the "Valley of the Kings" in Upper Egypt. Such mausoleums became de facto similar in value to the temple-palace complexes and, as such, were under the prophetic verdict of total destruction.

Jeremiah 7-10 is triggered by another "coming of the word of the Lord to Jeremiah" (7:1)[7] and adds further detail to the reason behind as well as the implementation of the divine punishment (8:4-9:25). It culminates with a diatribe against idols, the false gods that Judah chose over God (10:1-16), which is the ultimate reason behind God's indictment (vv.17-25). What holds the seemingly disparate passages together is the introductory verses that are constructed around the root *šub* and describe, in a

---

[7] This corresponds to the "'The word of the Lord came to me, saying" (2:1) that initiated chapters 2-6.

phraseology reminiscent of Isaiah 1:2-3,[8] Judah's attitude of disobedience:

> You shall say to them, Thus says the Lord: When men fall, do they not rise again? If one turns away (*yašub*), does he not return (*yašub*)? Why then has this people turned away (*šobebah*) in perpetual backsliding (*mešubbah*)? They hold fast to deceit, they refuse to return (*šub*). I have given heed and listened, but they have not spoken aright; no man repents of his wickedness, saying, "What have I done?" Every one turns (*šab*) to his own course, like a horse plunging headlong into battle. Even the stork in the heavens knows her times; and the turtledove, swallow, and crane keep the time of their coming; but my people know not the ordinance of the Lord. (Jer 8:4-7)

The recurrent use of the root *šub* is important on two levels. The first is auditory. This is an essential factor given that scripture was to be read aloud to an intended audience. In this particular case, the hearers are bombarded with a series of different words from the root *šub*, to which their attention is unequivocally drawn. What makes the matter even more impressive is that the connotation of *šub* is "turn (around)," "go in a different (opposite) direction" than the one the hearers were originally heading to. The corollary is that the same verb *šub* could mean "return" as well as "turn away." The most striking instance is "If one turns away (*yašub*), does he not return (*yašub*)?" (v.4b). The second reason for the importance of *šub* is that it is used by the author to invite the hearers to "return" to God after having "strayed away" from him so that, in turn, God would "turn

---

[8] "Hear, O heavens, and give ear, O earth; for the Lord has spoken: 'Sons have I reared and brought up, but they have rebelled against me. The ox knows its owner, and the ass its master's crib; but Israel does not know, my people does not understand.'"

again" his face to them after having "turned" his back to them. From the beginning, harlotry (the root *znh*), which a staple of the Book of Ezekiel, and rebellion (*peša'*), which is the basic depiction of Judah's disobedience at the outset of the Book of Isaiah, are cast in the *šub* terminology in Jeremiah:

> If a man divorces his wife and she goes from him and becomes another man's wife, will he return (*yašub*) to her? Would not that land be greatly polluted? You have played the harlot (*zanit*) with many lovers; and would you return (*šob*) to me? says the Lord … The Lord said to me in the days of King Josiah: "Have you seen what she did, that faithless one (*mešubbah*), Israel, how she went up on every high hill and under every green tree, and there played the harlot (*tizni*)? And I thought, 'After she has done all this she will return (*tašub*) to me'; but she did not return (*šabah*), and her false sister Judah saw it. She saw that for all the adulteries of that faithless one (*mešubbah*), Israel, I had sent her away with a decree of divorce; yet her false sister Judah did not fear, but she too went and played the harlot (*tizen*). Because harlotry (*zenut*) was so light to her, she polluted the land, committing adultery with stone and tree. Yet for all this her false sister Judah did not return (*šabah*) to me with her whole heart, but in pretense, says the Lord." And the Lord said to me, "Faithless (*mešubbah*) Israel has shown herself less guilty than false Judah. Go, and proclaim these words toward the north, and say, 'Return (*šubah*), faithless (*mešubbah*) Israel, says the Lord.' I will not look on you in anger, for I am merciful, says the Lord; I will not be angry for ever. Only acknowledge your guilt, that you rebelled (*paša'at*,) against the Lord your God and scattered your favors among strangers under every green tree, and that you have not obeyed my voice, says the Lord. Return (*šubu*), O faithless (*šobabim*) children, says the Lord; for I am your master; I will take you, one from a city and two from a family, and I will bring you to Zion … I thought how I would set you among my sons, and give you a pleasant land, a heritage most beauteous of all nations. And I thought 'you would call me, My Father, and would

not turn (*tašubi*) from following me.' ... Return (*šubu*), O faithless (*šobabim*) children, I will heal your faithlessness (*mešubot*). Behold, we come to thee; for thou art the Lord our God." (Jer 3:1, 6-14, 19, 22)

In order to understand the movement as well as the structure of the remainder of the content of "the word of the Lord that came to Jeremiah" (7:1) in 8:8-10:25, one is to remember that in the introductory chapter of the book, Jeremiah was "set this day over (*'al*; against)" not only Judah and Israel, but specifically "over (*'al*; against) nations and over kingdoms." The original actually has "over *the* nations and over *the* kingdoms"—among which are Israel and Judah—in order "to pluck up and to break down, to destroy and to overthrow, to build and to plant." (1:10) That both Israel and Judah are viewed as a "nation" just like any other nation is corroborated in the two instances that strikingly occur in the description of their "restored" status in conjunction with the new covenant:

> Thus says the Lord, who gives the sun for light by day and the fixed order of the moon and the stars for light by night, who stirs up the sea so that its waves roar— the Lord of hosts is his name: "If this fixed order departs from before me, says the Lord, then shall the descendants of Israel cease from being a nation (*goy*) before me for ever." (31:35-36)

> The word of the Lord came to Jeremiah: "Have you not observed what these people are saying, 'The Lord has rejected the two families which he chose'? Thus they have despised my people so that they are no longer a nation (*goy*) in their sight. Thus says the Lord: If I have not established my covenant with day and night and the ordinances of heaven and earth, then I will reject the descendants of Jacob and David my servant and will not choose one of his descendants to rule over the seed of Abraham, Isaac,

and Jacob. For I will restore their fortunes, and will have mercy upon them." (33:23-26)

The inclusion of the nations within the purview of the prophetic message is an essential feature of the Latter Prophets.[9] The exile, as one aspect of the punishment of the sinful sisters, Samaria and Jerusalem,[10] has scattered the "children" of those two cities among the nations so that the nations would hear and learn about the divine *mišpaṭ* (just judgment) and, by the same token, hear and learn about God's teaching inscribed in his *torah* (law), since the divine judgment was issued because the "children" did not abide by the Law:[11]

> Yet I will leave some of you alive. When you have among the nations some who escape the sword, and when you are scattered through the countries, then those of you who escape will remember me among the nations where they are carried captive, when I have broken their wanton heart which has departed from me, and blinded their eyes which turn wantonly after their idols; and they will be loathsome in their own sight for the evils which they have committed, for all their abominations. And they [the nations as well as the exiles][12] shall know that I am the Lord; I have not said in vain that I would do this evil to them. (Ezek 6:8-10)

> My servant David shall be king over them; and they shall all have one shepherd. They shall follow my ordinances and be careful to observe my statutes. They shall dwell in the land where your fathers dwelt that I gave to my servant Jacob; they and their

---

[9] I have shown this repeatedly in my commentaries on Ezekiel and Isaiah.
[10] E.g., Jer 15:2; 21:7-9; 27:13; Ezek 5:12-17; 7:15; 12:14-16.
[11] The other three being death by sword, famine, or sickness during the siege; see Jer 6:19; 9:13.
[12] See my comments in *C-Ezek* 109-11.

children and their children's children shall dwell there for ever; and David my servant shall be their prince for ever. I will make a covenant of peace with them; it shall be an everlasting covenant with them; and I will bless them and multiply them, and will set my sanctuary in the midst of them for evermore. My dwelling place shall be with them; and I will be their God, and they shall be my people. Then the nations will know that I the Lord sanctify Israel, when my sanctuary is in the midst of them for evermore. (37:24-28)

Behold my servant, whom I uphold, my chosen, in whom my soul delights; I have put my Spirit upon him, he will bring forth justice (*mišpaṭ*) to the nations. He will not cry or lift up his voice, or make it heard in the street; a bruised reed he will not break, and a dimly burning wick he will not quench; he will faithfully bring forth justice (*mišpaṭ*). He will not fail or be discouraged till he has established justice (*mišpaṭ*) in the earth; and the coastlands wait for his law (*torah*). Thus says God, the Lord, who created the heavens and stretched them out, who spread forth the earth and what comes from it, who gives breath to the people upon it and spirit to those who walk in it: I am the Lord, I have called you in righteousness, I have taken you by the hand and kept you; I have given you as a covenant to the people, a light to the nations, to open the eyes that are blind, to bring out the prisoners from the dungeon, from the prison those who sit in darkness. (Is 42:1-7)

This teaching is reflected in the structure of Jeremiah as well. Verses 8:8-9:25 contain a detailed description of Jerusalem's sins of disobedience which leads to the issuance of the divine verdict of its destruction (8:10-9:21). These verses are bracketed by two passages underscoring that true wisdom lies in the knowledge of God's law and its implementation:

> How can you say, "We are wise, and the law of the Lord is with us"? But behold, the false pen of the scribes (*sopherim*) has made it

into a lie. The wise men shall be put to shame, they shall be dismayed and taken; lo, they have rejected the word of the Lord, and what wisdom is in them? (8:8-9)

Thus says the Lord: "Let not the wise man glory in his wisdom, let not the mighty man glory in his might, let not the rich man glory in his riches; but let him who glories glory in this, that he understands and knows me, that I am the Lord who practice steadfast love (*ḥesed*), justice (*mišpaṭ*), and righteousness (*ṣedaqah*) in the earth; for in these things I delight, says the Lord." (9:23-24)

The view of the Law as true wisdom is a staple of the third part of the Old Testament, the Writings (*ketubim*), whose function is to prod Israel to share the Law with the wisdom seeking nations.[13] The Book of Job is the quintessential representative of that literature. Job was a devout Jew who was born, lived, and died outside Canaan, that is to say, among the nations, and yet abided by the dictates of the Law.

As Moses had instructed (Deut 17:18; 31:39),[14] the Law was entrusted to the priests (Jer 2:8; 18:18) who were supposed to share its wisdom with the people in their charge (8:8a). However, since the priests of the temple of Jerusalem failed in their duty and falsified its teaching (8:8b), the true content of that same Law was entrusted to Jeremiah to be delivered again as "the word of the Lord" (8:9b). God proceeded to accomplish through Jeremiah the prophet what he had earlier done through Moses the prophet: after having delivered that "word" as "words" (1:1, 9) into the ears of all

---

[13] See *OTI₃* 157-9.
[14] See also Josh 3:3, 14, 17; 8:33.

those who approach the gates of that temple,[15] Jeremiah will have those same words consigned to a scroll by "Baruch the scribe (*sopher*)" (36:32). That the author already had in mind chapter 36 is evident from the fact that before that chapter the noun *sopher* occurs only in 8:8 and refers, no less, to the priests of Jerusalem, Jeremiah's opponents (1:18; 26:7-11). Furthermore, the Book of Jeremiah was meant ultimately to be shared not only with the Judahite exiles to whom Jeremiah wrote a letter (29:1-3), but also with the nations where exiles were scattered. Such an intention can be gathered from the end bracket of the divine indictment against Judah (9:23-24) where the rich and powerful, representative of the nations that overran Judah with their might, are included with the vain "wise man" (10:17-24). [16] Despite their might they "did not know the Lord" (v.25) as one is supposed to (9:24), and thus fell prey to their own arrogance. This finds full corroboration in what appears to be an out-of-context ending of chapter 9:

> Behold, the days are coming, says the Lord, when I will punish all those who are circumcised but yet uncircumcised—Egypt, Judah, Edom, the sons of Ammon, Moab, and all who dwell in the desert that cut the corners of their hair; for all these nations are uncircumcised, and all the house of Israel is uncircumcised in heart. (vv.25-26)

What is the function of such an "additional comment" regarding circumcision? The only other reference to circumcision in the book

---

[15] "Stand in the gate of the Lord's house, and proclaim there this word, and say, *Hear* the word of the Lord, all you men of Judah who enter these gates to worship the Lord." (7:2)

[16] Paul will use Jer 9:23-24 to level his criticism against the arrogance of both the Corinthians and his opponents in 1 Cor 1:26-31; see my comments in *C-1Cor* 47-8.

occurred earlier in an address to Judah and Jerusalem in these terms:

> "If you return, O Israel, says the Lord, to me you should return. If you remove your abominations from my presence, and do not waver, and if you swear, 'As the Lord lives,' in truth (*'emet*), in justice (*mišpaṭ*), and in uprightness (*ṣedaqah*), then nations shall bless themselves in him, and in him shall they glory." For thus says the Lord to the men of Judah and to the inhabitants of Jerusalem: "Break up your fallow ground, and sow not among thorns. Circumcise yourselves to the Lord, remove the foreskin of your hearts, O men of Judah and inhabitants of Jerusalem; lest my wrath go forth like fire, and burn with none to quench it, because of the evil of your doings." (4:1-4)

The intended connection between these two passages (4:1-4 and 9:23-26) is manifest in the similar terminology. Not only do we encounter the only instances of circumcision in Jeremiah, but also circumcision is defined as acting in accord with the divine will. Just as God "practices steadfast love (*ḥesed*), justice (*mišpaṭ*), and righteousness (*ṣedaqah*) in the earth" (9:24), those who return to him (4:1) and get to know him truly, that is, know his will (9:24) are to behave "in truth (*'emet*), in justice (*mišpaṭ*), and in uprightness (*ṣedaqah*)" (4:2), that is, to be "after God's heart."[17] Consequently, the circumcision required by God as a sign that one pertains to his "household" is not a matter of the flesh, but a matter of the heart (Hebrew *leb*), which is the "core" of one's being, the center that controls one's behavior and actions as well as one's thoughts and feelings. That is why God's request through

---

[17] See, e.g., Jer 15:1: "Then the Lord said to me, 'Though Moses and Samuel stood before me, yet my heart would not turn toward this people. Send them out of my sight, and let them go!'"

Jeremiah (4:1-4) is none other than his original request through Moses:

> And now, Israel, what does the Lord your God require of you, but to fear the Lord your God, to walk in all his ways, to love him, to serve the Lord your God with all your heart and with all your soul, and to keep the commandments and statutes of the Lord, which I command you this day for your good? Behold, to the Lord your God belong heaven and the heaven of heavens, the earth with all that is in it; yet the Lord set his heart in love upon your fathers and chose their descendants after them, you above all peoples, as at this day. Circumcise therefore the foreskin of your heart, and be no longer stubborn. For the Lord your God is God of gods and Lord of lords, the great, the mighty, and the terrible God, who is not partial and takes no bribe. He executes (*'oŝeh*) justice (*mišpaṭ*) for the fatherless (*yatom*) and the widow (*'almanah*), and loves the sojourner (*ger*), giving him food and clothing. Love the sojourner therefore; for you were sojourners in the land of Egypt. (Deut 10:12-19)

The harsh punishment against Judah and Jerusalem in Jeremiah 7:12-15 is due to their neglect of the divine request:

> For if you truly amend your ways and your doings, if you truly (*'aśo*) execute (*ta'aśu*) justice (*mišpaṭ*) one with another, if you do not oppress the alien (*ger*), the fatherless (*yatom*) or the widow (*'almanah*), or shed innocent blood in this place, and if you do not go after other gods to your own hurt, then I will let you dwell in this place, in the land that I gave of old to your fathers for ever. (7:5-7)

Whenever they do not abide by God's law they end up being as "uncircumcised" as the nations *around* them. Notice how, at the end of chapter 9, not only is the house of Israel on the same level as the nations, but also Judah is intentionally thrown in the midst of the surrounding nations, squeezed between Egypt and Edom: "Behold, the days are coming, says the Lord, when I will punish all those who are circumcised but yet uncircumcised—Egypt, Judah, Edom, the sons of Ammon, Moab, and all who dwell in the desert that cut the corners of their hair; for all these nations are uncircumcised, and all the house of Israel is uncircumcised in heart." (vv.25-26)

It is precisely at this juncture (chapter 10) that we hear a long harangue against the gods of the nations. Its purpose is to confirm that the Lord who intended to include the uncircumcised nations in his covenant of circumcision (Gen 17:9-14) is the same God who promulgated the Law and is the sole valid deity for the nations as well as for Israel. Should the nations not "know" him, that is, know his will inscribed in that Law and abide by it, they would incur God's wrath just as Israel did: "Pour out thy wrath upon the nations (*goyim*) that know thee not, and upon the peoples (*mišpaḥot*; families [clans]) that call not on thy name." (Jer 10:25a) It is worthwhile to note that the choice of "families" (*mišpaḥot*) as parallel to nations (*goyim*) here is deliberate and brings to mind the preceding occurrence of that noun used in conjunction with the harsh condemnation of the kingly mausoleums:

> At that time, says the Lord, the bones of the kings of Judah, the bones of its princes, the bones of the priests, the bones of the prophets, and the bones of the inhabitants of Jerusalem shall be brought out of their tombs; and they shall be spread before the sun and the moon and all the host of heaven, which they have loved and served, which they have gone after, and which they have sought and worshiped; and they shall not be gathered or buried;

they shall be as dung on the surface of the ground. Death shall be preferred to life by all the remnant that remains of this evil family (*mišpaḥah*) in all the places where I have driven them, says the Lord of hosts. (8:1-3)[18]

---

[18] The author's intentionality is corroborated in that these are the only instances of *mišpaḥah* in the section 7:1-10:25 introduced with the second "coming of the word of the Lord to Jeremiah" (7:1).

Chapter 4
The Covenant of the Lord

The third "coming of the Lord's word" to Jeremiah (11:1) covers chapters 11-15. It is basically an expansion of what was heard in chapter 7 concerning obedience to the "voice" of God. It is cast in terms of a "covenant" in view of the "new covenant" (31:31-34), which will be announced in Jeremiah's "Book of Consolation" (chs.30-33). With the exception of the phrase "the ark of the covenant" (3:16), the noun "covenant" occurs five times within ten verses at the start of chapter 11 (vv.2, 3, 6, 8, 10), and appears again with a high frequency in chapters 30-33 (31:31, 32, 33; 32:40; 33:20, 21, 25). So, from its outset, chapter 11 prepares for as well as justifies the need for the re-institution of the covenant that has been broken,[1] which will give another and final chance for the hearers to *become* God's people and, by the same token, for the Lord to *become* their God:

> The word that came to Jeremiah from the Lord: "Hear the words of this covenant, and speak to the men of Judah and the inhabitants of Jerusalem. You shall say to them, Thus says the Lord, the God of Israel: Cursed be the man who does not heed the words of this covenant which I commanded your fathers when I brought them out of the land of Egypt, from the iron furnace, saying, Listen to my voice, and do all that I command you. So shall you be my people, and I will be your God, that I may perform the oath which I swore to your fathers, to give them a land flowing with milk and honey, as at this day." Then I answered, "So be it, Lord." And the Lord said to me, "Proclaim all

---
[1] Jer 14:21 and 22:9 refer to the breaking of that covenant.

these words in the cities of Judah, and in the streets of Jerusalem: Hear the words of this covenant and do them. For I solemnly warned your fathers when I brought them up out of the land of Egypt, warning them persistently, even to this day, saying, Obey my voice. Yet they did not obey or incline their ear, but every one walked in the stubbornness of his evil heart. Therefore I brought upon them all the words of this covenant, which I commanded them to do, but they did not." (11:1-8)

This teaching corresponds to that of Ezekiel:

And the Spirit of the Lord fell upon me, and he said to me, "Say, Thus says the Lord: So you think, O house of Israel; for I know the things that come into your mind. You have multiplied your slain in this city, and have filled its streets with the slain. Therefore thus says the Lord God: Your slain whom you have laid in the midst of it, they are the flesh, and this city is the caldron; but you shall be brought forth out of the midst of it. You have feared the sword; and I will bring the sword upon you, says the Lord God. And I will bring you forth out of the midst of it, and give you into the hands of foreigners, and execute judgments upon you. You shall fall by the sword; I will judge you at the border of Israel; and you shall know that I am the Lord. This city shall not be your caldron, nor shall you be the flesh in the midst of it; I will judge you at the border of Israel; and you shall know that I am the Lord; for you have not walked in my statutes, nor executed my ordinances, but have acted according to the ordinances of the nations that are round about you." ... And the word of the Lord came to me: "Son of man, your brethren, even your brethren, your fellow exiles, the whole house of Israel, all of them, are those of whom the inhabitants of Jerusalem have said, 'They have gone far from the Lord; to us this land is given for a possession.' Therefore say, 'Thus says the Lord God: Though I removed them far off among the nations, and though I scattered them among the countries, yet I have been a sanctuary to them for a while in the countries where they have gone.' Therefore say,

'Thus says the Lord God: I will gather you from the peoples, and assemble you out of the countries where you have been scattered, and I will give you the land of Israel.' And when they come there, they will remove from it all its detestable things and all its abominations. And I will give them one heart, and put a new spirit within them; I will take the stony heart out of their flesh and give them a heart of flesh, that they may walk in my statutes and keep my ordinances and obey them; *and they shall be my people, and I will be their God*. But as for those whose heart goes after their detestable things and their abominations, I will requite their deeds upon their own heads, says the Lord God." (11:5-12, 14-21)

Later the same thought is cast in terms of a "new covenant":

> I will make with them a covenant of peace and banish wild beasts from the land, so that they may dwell securely in the wilderness and sleep in the woods ... They shall no more be a prey to the nations, nor shall the beasts of the land devour them; they shall dwell securely, and none shall make them afraid. And I will provide for them prosperous plantations so that they shall no more be consumed with hunger in the land, and no longer suffer the reproach of the nations. And they shall know that I, the Lord their God, am with them, and that *they*, the house of Israel, *are my people*, says the Lord God. And you are my sheep, the sheep of my pasture, and *I am your God*, says the Lord God. (34:25, 28-31)

> I will make a covenant of peace with them; it shall be an everlasting covenant with them; and I will bless them and multiply them, and will set my sanctuary in the midst of them for evermore. My dwelling place shall be with them; and *I will be their God*, and *they shall be my people*. (37:26-27)

It is important to recognize that the central terms in the author's purview have an "itinerary" or "trajectory" which is to be followed in order for the hearers to understand what the author is saying.² Put otherwise, the true understanding of the "meaning" of a term lies in the function that term has in the book's movement or "story." Furthermore, the "trajectories" of two different terms can be intertwined and their respective functions are to be grasped together. In the case of Jeremiah, the "trajectory" of "covenant" is closely linked to that of the "voice" of the Lord. What makes this connection even more impressive is that the first occurrence of "voice" (3:11-14) looks forward to 31:31-34 concerning the new covenant. Furthermore, 3:11-14 is constructed around the root *šub*, a staple of the Book of Jeremiah. All of these features make of 3:11-14 an axial passage containing the basic message that will be developed throughout the book. It is precisely here that the hearer encounters for the first time the "voice" (*qol*) of the Lord and "(not) obeying that voice," to boot, which is also a staple of Jeremiah:³

> And the Lord said to me, "Faithless Israel has shown herself less guilty than false Judah. Go, and proclaim these words toward the north, and say, 'Return, faithless Israel,' says the Lord. I will not look on you in anger, for I am merciful, says the Lord; I will not be angry for ever. Only acknowledge your guilt, that you rebelled against the Lord your God and scattered your favors among strangers under every green tree, and that you have not obeyed my voice (*qol*), says the Lord. Return, O faithless children, says the Lord; for I am your master; I will take you, one from a city and two from a family, and I will bring you to Zion." (3:11-14)

---

[2] I repeatedly showed this in my commentary on Ezekiel.
[3] 3:13, 25; 7:23, 28; 9:13; 11:4 (RSV has "listen to" for the same original *šama' be*); 11:7; 18:10 (RSV has "listen to" for the same original *šama' be*); 22:21; 26:13; 32:23; 38:20; 40:3; 42:6 [twice], 13, 21; 43:4, 7; 44:23.

After this appeal and immediately following God's invitation to "Return (*šubu*), O faithless (*šobabim*) sons, I will heal your faithlessness (*šubot*)" (v.22a),[4] one hears the people confess that they were deserving the divine punishment since they "have not obeyed the voice of the Lord our God":

> Behold, we come to thee; for thou art the Lord our God. Truly the hills are a delusion, the orgies on the mountains. Truly in the Lord our God is the salvation of Israel. But from our youth the shameful thing has devoured all for which our fathers labored, their flocks and their herds, their sons and their daughters. Let us lie down in our shame, and let our dishonor cover us; for we have sinned against the Lord our God, we and our fathers, from our youth even to this day; and we have not obeyed the voice of the Lord our God. (vv.22b-25)

The subsequent instance of "obeying the Lord's voice" (7:21-29) elaborates on the value of that directive:

> [21]Thus says the Lord of hosts, the God of Israel: "Add your burnt offerings to your sacrifices, and eat the flesh. [22]For in the day that I brought them out of the land of Egypt, I did not speak to your fathers or command them concerning burnt offerings and sacrifices. [23]But this command I gave them, 'Obey my voice, and I will be your God, and you shall be my people; and walk in all the way that I command you, that it may be well with you.' [24]But they did not obey or incline their ear, but walked in their own counsels and the stubbornness of their evil hearts, and went backward and not forward. [25]From the day that your fathers came out of the land of Egypt to this day, I have persistently sent all my servants the prophets to them, day after day; [26]yet they did not listen to me, or incline their ear, but stiffened their neck. They did worse than their fathers. [27]So you shall speak all these words to them, but they

---

[4] See my comments on the root *šub* earlier on pp. 47-48.

will not listen to you. You shall call to them, but they will not answer you. ²⁸And you shall say to them, 'This is the nation that did not obey the voice of the Lord their God, and did not accept discipline (*musar*); truth has perished; it is cut off from their lips. ²⁹Cut off your hair and cast it away; raise a lamentation on the bare heights, for the Lord has rejected and forsaken the generation of his wrath.'"

An analysis of this passage will show its value not only for the Book of Jeremiah, but also for the entire scripture.

As previously pointed out, chapters 2-6 and 7-10 form two sections each introduced by a coming of the word of the Lord to Jeremiah. Early on in each there is a reference to the voice of the Lord that was not heeded (3:11-14; 7:21-29). In the latter case (7:21-23) one has the distinct impression that the Lord's voice is pitted against the express commandments of the Law. However, such an impression soon dissipates when two chapters later one hears of a full equivalence between the Law and the Lord's voice:

> And the Lord says: "Because they have forsaken my law which I set before them, and have not obeyed my voice, or walked in accord with it, but have stubbornly followed their own hearts and have gone after the Baals, as their fathers taught them. Therefore thus says the Lord of hosts, the God of Israel: Behold, I will feed this people with wormwood, and give them poisonous water to drink. I will scatter them among the nations whom neither they nor their fathers have known; and I will send the sword after them, until I have consumed them." (9:13-16)

Recalling 7:21-29, one will soon notice that there the voice of the Lord was communicated through the "prophets" he kept sending after the issuance of the Law (vv.26-27). Furthermore, the attentive hearers, who are trained in "listening to" the Old Testament scriptures in their canonical sequence—Law,

The Covenant of the Lord

Prophets (Prior [Joshua, Judges, Samuel, Kings] and Latter [Isaiah, Jeremiah, Ezekiel, the Scroll of the Twelve Prophets]), Writings—will realize that the text of Jeremiah is aiming at the canonization of scripture in this order. In other words, the Book of Jeremiah is pivotal in that it is (1) canonizing the Prophets, the second part of the Old Testament, *as scripture* and thus putting it on the same level of authority as the Law, and (2) setting up the case for the canonization of the Writings as well. This reading is corroborated in the following features of the text.

Instruction (musar)

In 7:28 the teaching through the voice of the Lord is referred to as "instruction" (*musar*). An overview of this noun in scripture will reveal that Jeremiah is the bridge between the Law and the Writings. The term occurs only once in the five books of the Law in the following context: "You shall therefore love the Lord your God, and keep his charge, his statutes, his ordinances, and his commandments always. And consider this day (since I am not speaking to your children who have not known or seen it), consider the discipline (*musar*; instruction) of the Lord your God, his greatness, his mighty hand and his outstretched arm." (Deut 11:1-2) It is noticeable that after the death of the generation that left Egypt the Law was re-issued at Mount Nebo specifically as instruction for the new generation about to enter Canaan. Later their children would receive that same "instruction" in God's will through the generations of "prophets" who would make the "voice" of the Lord resound, beginning with the Book of Joshua (8:32-35; 24:1-28)[5]: "And the people said to Joshua, 'The Lord our God we will serve, and

---

[5] My readers are reminded that the Book of Joshua is the first book in the second part of the Old Testament scripture, the Prophets.

his voice we will obey.'" (24:24) The noun *musar*, however, does not appear after Deuteronomy 11:2 until the Book of Jeremiah,[6] where it occurs frequently. After Jeremiah one hears of *musar* only in Zephaniah 3:2 and 7.[7] Upon reviewing the instances of *musar* in Jeremiah one will notice that they are intended to lead up to the scripturalization of Jeremiah's teaching in chapter 36. In other words, Jeremiah's words—God's words through Jeremiah (1:9b)—are as much *musar* to the following generations of hearers as the Law of Moses (Deut 11:2).

In chapters 2-6 that covered the first coming of the Lord's word to Jeremiah (2:1), we heard twice (2:30 and 5:3) that the divine *musar*, as punitive correction, was disregarded by the people. In between those two instances the people are summoned to acknowledge their wrong doing as disobedience to the Lord's voice, a summons to which they comply:

> Only acknowledge your guilt, that you rebelled against the Lord your God and scattered your favors among strangers under every green tree, and that you have not obeyed my voice, says the Lord. (3:13)

> Let us lie down in our shame, and let our dishonor cover us; for we have sinned against the Lord our God, we and our fathers,

---

[6] Is 17:1 and 53:5 (in Hebrew) are no exceptions. Neither instance applies to the teaching of the Law. The first is the title of the oracle addressed to Tyre; the second refers to the chastisement inflicted on the Lord's servant for our sins' sake.

[7] Ezek 5:15 and Hos 5:2 are no exceptions. The first refers to the chastisement of Jerusalem as a warning example for the nations: "You shall be a reproach and a taunt, a warning (*musar*) and a horror, to the nations round about you, when I execute judgments on you in anger and fury, and with furious chastisements." The second refers metaphorically to God as a chastisement to the house of Israel: "And they have made deep the pit of Shittim, but I *will chastise* (*musar*, [am; shall be] a chastisement to) all of them."

The Covenant of the Lord

from our youth even to this day; and we have not obeyed the voice of the Lord our God. (3:25)

Following the second coming of the Lord's word to Jeremiah (7:1), the Judahites are chastened for having disobeyed the *musar* communicated to them by the "voice of the Lord" through the words of Jeremiah:

> So you shall speak all these words to them, but they will not listen to you. You shall call to them, but they will not answer you. And you shall say to them, "This is the nation that did not obey the voice of the Lord their God, and did not accept discipline (*musar*); truth has perished; it is cut off from their lips." (7:27-28)

In this passage the same voice of the Lord is tantamount to the Law. Those disobedient to that voice will be punished with the exile among the nations, a punishment declared through the mouth of Jeremiah (9:13-16). Moreover, in their land of exile the people are not to follow the *musar* of the idols who are "but wood" (10:8), rather they are to abide by the *musar* of the Law and, as we shall see, that of the Jeremianic scripture (ch.36), which *musar* would be imparted to them on the sabbath gatherings when scripture is read aloud:[8]

> Thus said the Lord to me: "Go and stand in the Benjamin Gate, by which the kings of Judah enter and by which they go out, and in all the gates of Jerusalem, and say: 'Hear the word of the Lord, you kings of Judah, and all Judah, and all the inhabitants of Jerusalem, who enter by these gates. Thus says the Lord: Take heed for the sake of your lives, and do not bear a burden on the sabbath day or bring it in by the gates of Jerusalem. And do not carry a burden out of your houses on the sabbath or do any work,

---

[8] See my comments in *C-Ezek* 225-57 where I also discuss the fact that the sabbath institution arose during the exile.

but keep the sabbath day holy, as I commanded your fathers. Yet they did not listen or incline their ear, but stiffened their neck, that they might not hear and receive instruction (*musar*)." (17:19-23)

In the Book of Consolation (chs.30-34) the teaching concerning *musar* is underscored: whenever the divine *musar* as guiding instruction goes unheeded (32:33) the Lord's anger is provoked (v.32), and the same *musar* turns into an instructional punishment (30:14), as delineated in the Law that portends curses as well as blessings (Lev 26 and Deut 28). It is precisely at this point and before chapter 36, that one encounters *musar* for the last time in Jeremiah in an interesting chapter regarding the Rechabites who are given as an example for the Judahites to follow. The Rechabites obeyed the "words" (*debarim*) and "command(ment)" (*miṣwah*) of their father, a mere human, while the Judahites did not receive the instruction (*musar*) of God himself nor did they listen to his words (*debarim*):

> [12]Then the word of the Lord came to Jeremiah: [13]"Thus says the Lord of hosts, the God of Israel: Go and say to the men of Judah and the inhabitants of Jerusalem, Will you not receive instruction (*musar*) and listen to my words (*debarim*)? says the Lord. [14]The command (*debarim*; words) which Jonadab the son of Rechab *gave* (*ṣiwwah*; commanded) to his sons, to drink no wine, has been kept; and they drink none to this day, for they have obeyed their father's command (*miṣwah*). I have spoken to you persistently, but you have not listened to me. [15]I have sent to you all my servants the prophets, sending them persistently, saying, 'Turn now every one of you from his evil way, and amend your doings, and do not go after other gods to serve them, and then you shall dwell in the land which I gave to you and your fathers.' But you did not incline your ear or listen to me. [16]The sons of Jonadab the son of Rechab have kept the command (*miṣwah*) which their father gave

(*ṣiwwah*; commanded) them, but this people has not obeyed me. ¹⁷Therefore, thus says the Lord, the God of hosts, the God of Israel: Behold, I am bringing on Judah and all the inhabitants of Jerusalem all the evil that I have pronounced against them; because I have spoken to them and they have not listened, I have called to them and they have not answered." (Jer 35)

Notice, on the one hand, how the original plays on the parallelism between the "words" of the Lord (v.13) and the "words" of Jonadab (v.14) that were issued as a "command(ment)" (vv.14 and 16), which is precisely Law terminology. Notice, on the other hand, that the divine "words" in this case are those God uttered as "instruction" (*musar*) through "his prophets," among whom is Jeremiah. This harks back to chapter 7:

> From the day that your fathers came out of the land of Egypt to this day, I have persistently sent *all my servants the prophets* to them, day after day; yet they did not listen to me, or incline their ear, but stiffened their neck. They did worse than their fathers. So *you shall speak all these words* to them, but they will not listen to you. You shall call to them, but they will not answer you. And you shall say to them, 'This is the nation that did not obey the voice of the Lord their God, and did not accept discipline (*musar*; instruction); truth has perished; it is cut off from their lips'. (vv.25-28)

It is obedience to the command expressed in words that will ensure the divine blessing. Such can be seen in that, as of now, the Rechabites are granted what is promised to Judah if Judah obeys the will of God when granted the second chance through the new covenant (31:31-34):

> But to the house of the Rechabites Jeremiah said, "Thus says the Lord of hosts, the God of Israel: Because you have obeyed the

command of Jonadab your father, and kept all his precepts, and done all that he commanded you, therefore thus says the Lord of hosts, the God of Israel: Jonadab the son of Rechab shall never lack a man to stand before me." (35:18-19)

Behold, the days are coming, says the Lord, when I will fulfil the promise I made to the house of Israel and the house of Judah. In those days and at that time I will cause a righteous Branch to spring forth for David; and he shall execute justice and righteousness in the land. In those days Judah will be saved and Jerusalem will dwell securely. And this is the name by which it will be called: "The Lord is our righteousness." For thus says the Lord: David shall never lack a man to sit on the throne of the house of Israel, and the Levitical priests shall never lack a man in my presence to offer burnt offerings, to burn cereal offerings, and to make sacrifices for ever. (33:14-18)

These are the only three instances of "shall never lack a man" (*lo' yikkaret 'iš*; shall not be cut out a man) in Jeremiah.

Once the equivalence has been established between the Law and the prophetic "words" in the matter of securing the divine blessing for those who would obey the "voice" and the "words" of God, chapter 36 seals that equivalence for all upcoming generations by scripturalizing into a scroll the "words" of the Lord that he put into the mouth of Jeremiah (1:9). The scriptural school of authors deftly expanded the scripturalization of Jeremiah to include the entire corpus of the Latter Prophets,[9] and by extension, of the Prophets (Prior[10] as well as Latter), by using *musar* (instruction) twice in tandem in Zephaniah 3:2 and 7 in a setting reminiscent of Jeremiah's teaching:

---

[9] Isaiah, Jeremiah, Ezekiel, and the Scroll of the Twelve Prophets.
[10] Joshua, Judges, Samuel, and Kings.

Woe to her that is rebellious and defiled, the oppressing city! She listens to no voice, she accepts (*laqeḥah*; from the verb *laqaḥ* [receive]) no correction (*musar*). She does not trust in the Lord, she does not draw near to her God. Her officials within her are roaring lions; her judges are evening wolves that leave nothing till the morning. Her prophets are wanton, faithless men; her priests profane what is sacred, they do violence to the law. The Lord within her is righteous, he does no wrong; every morning he shows forth his justice, each dawn he does not fail; but the unjust knows no shame. I have cut off nations; their battlements are in ruins; I have laid waste their streets so that none walks in them; their cities have been made desolate, without a man, without an inhabitant. I said, "Surely she will fear me, she will accept (*tiqḥi*; from the verb *laqaḥ* [receive]) correction (*musar*); she will not lose sight of all that I have enjoined upon her." But all the more they were eager to make all their deeds corrupt." (Zeph 3:1-7)

Notice even the correspondence in phraseology; we find the same phrase *laqaḥ musar* in Jeremiah 5:3 (take correction); 7:28 (accept discipline); 17:23 (receive instruction); 32:33 (receive instruction); 35:13 (receive instruction), a phrase not encountered in Isaiah (17:11; 53:5), Ezekiel (5:15), and Hosea (5:2) where *musar* occurs.[11] It is only in Zephaniah, a contemporary of Jeremiah who is said to have prophesied "in the days of Josiah the son of Amon, king of Judah" (Zeph 1:1), as did Jeremiah (Jer 1:2). Furthermore, canonically, these two prophets are presented as the last ones to be active in Jerusalem that was about to fall, since they are followed by an exilic prophet (Ezekiel) in the case of Jeremiah, or by post-exilic prophets (Haggai, Zachariah, Malachi) in the case of Zephaniah.

---

[11] I am referring here to the Hebrew original.

Beyond the Prophets, the second part of the Old Testament scripture, *musar* is already planting in the mind of the hearers the scripturalization of the third part of that scripture, the Writings (*ketubim*). Indeed, upon listening to the book of "the Proverbs of Solomon," the third book of the Writings after Psalms and Job, even a not so attentive hearer will be struck by both the frequent occurrence of *musar* and its parallelism with *torah* (law) in the opening verses:

> The proverbs of Solomon, son of David, king of Israel: That men may know wisdom and instruction (*musar*), understand words of insight, receive instruction (*musar*) in wise dealing, righteousness, justice, and equity ... The fear of the Lord is the beginning of knowledge; fools despise wisdom and instruction (*musar*). Hear, my son, your father's instruction (*musar*), and reject not your mother's teaching (*torah*); for they are a fair garland for your head, and pendants for your neck. (Prov 1:1-3; 7-9)

The initial impression concerning the centrality of *musar* will turn into conviction since Proverbs has by far the highest incidence of that noun in the entire scripture: 31 times compared to a total of 20 instances in the rest of scripture, eight of which occur in Jeremiah. So the Book of Jeremiah is imposing upon his hearers the reality of the tripartite Old Testament scripture, which finds its most concise and official expression in the prologue to Ecclesiasticus, the Wisdom of Sirach:

> Whereas many great teachings have been given to us through *the law and the prophets and the others that followed them*, on account of which we should praise Israel for instruction (*paideia*) and wisdom; and since it is necessary not only that the readers themselves should acquire understanding but also that those who love learning should be able to help the outsiders by both speaking and writing, my grandfather Jesus, after devoting himself especially to the reading of *the law and the prophets and the other*

books of our fathers, and after acquiring considerable proficiency in them, was himself also led to write something pertaining to *instruction* and wisdom, in order that, by becoming conversant with this also, those who love learning should make even greater progress in living according to the law.

You are urged therefore to read with good will and attention, and to be indulgent in cases where, despite our diligent labor in translating, we may seem to have rendered some phrases imperfectly. For what was originally expressed in Hebrew does not have exactly the same sense when translated into another language. Not only this work, but even *the law itself, the prophecies, and the rest of the books* differ not a little as originally expressed.

When I came to Egypt in the thirty-eighth year of the reign of Euergetes and stayed for some time, I found opportunity for no little instruction (*paideia*). It seemed highly necessary that I should myself devote some pains and labor to the translation of the following book, using in that period of time great watchfulness and skill in order to complete and publish the book for those living abroad who wished to gain learning, being prepared in character to live according to the law.[12]

It is important to note here in this regard that the Greek word *paideia* in the Prologue to Sirach is precisely the same word that the LXX uses to render the Hebrew *musar* in Proverbs 1:1-9[13] as well as in Jeremiah 2:30; 5:3; 7:28;17:23; 30:14; 32:33; 35:13 and in Zephaniah 3:2 and 7.

Moses and Samuel

This finding regarding *musar* is sealed in a particularly striking feature of the Lord's word to Jeremiah in chapter 15:

---

[12] See my comments in *OTI₃* 143-46.
[13] The same applies virtually to all occurrences of *musar* in that book.

> Then the Lord said to me, "Though Moses and Samuel stood before me, yet my heart would not turn toward this people. Send them out of my sight, and let them go! And when they ask you, 'Where shall we go?' you shall say to them, 'Thus says the Lord: Those who are for pestilence, to pestilence, and those who are for the sword, to the sword; those who are for famine, to famine, and those who are for captivity, to captivity.'" (vv.1-2)

This statement on the Lord's part is to underscore that his decision is final, just as he said earlier to Jeremiah: "As for you, do not pray for this people, or lift up cry or prayer for them, and do not intercede with me, for I do not hear you." (7:16) However, there is much more here than strikes the ear in this virtually unique combination of Moses and Samuel, which is exclusive to Jeremiah 15:1 and Psalm 99:6 in the entire scripture in both its Testaments. Its function is multi-faceted.

First of all, it is clearly intended to support the rationale behind the divine verdict communicated through Jeremiah: "From the day that your fathers came out of the land of Egypt to this day, I have persistently sent all my servants the prophets to them, day after day; yet they did not listen to me, or incline their ear, but stiffened their neck. They did worse than their fathers." (Jer 7:25-26) Moses and Samuel are the first two "prophets of the Lord" in scripture: "And there has not arisen a prophet since in Israel like Moses, whom the Lord knew face to face" (Deut 34:10); "And all Israel from Dan to Beer-sheba knew that Samuel was established as a prophet of the Lord. And the Lord appeared again at Shiloh, for the Lord revealed himself to Samuel at Shiloh by the word of the Lord. And the word of Samuel came to all Israel." (1 Sam 3:20-4:1a) The inclusion of Samuel with Moses is thus very à propos considering the reference to Shiloh earlier in Jeremiah's invective against the temple (7:12, 14).

Secondly, these two prophets function as representatives of the Law and the Prior Prophets. This is corroborated by a similar instance at the end of Malachi where it is Elijah who functions a stand-in for the Prior Prophets: "Remember the law of my servant Moses, the statutes and ordinances that I commanded him at Horeb for all Israel. Behold, I will send you Elijah the prophet before the great and terrible day of the Lord comes. And he will turn the hearts of fathers to their children and the hearts of children to their fathers, lest I come and smite the land with a curse." (4:4-6) By referring to Moses, Samuel and Elijah, both Jeremiah and Malachi establish the Latter Prophets as scripture in the same vein as the Law and the Prior Prophets. However, just as was the case with *musar*, it is Jeremiah's terminology that builds the bridge toward the inclusion of the Writings in the scriptural canon. Indeed, in Psalms, the first and thus representative book of that corpus, we find the only other instance of Moses and Samuel together in scripture:

> Moses and Aaron were among his priests, Samuel also was among those who called on his name. They cried to the Lord, and he answered them. He spoke to them in the pillar of cloud; they kept his testimonies, and the statutes that he gave them. O Lord our God, thou didst answer them; thou wast a forgiving God to them, but an avenger of their wrongdoings.[14] (99:6-8)

The closeness to Jeremiah's message is evident in that, although God accepts the intercessions of Moses and Samuel, he remains

---

[14] The original Hebrew, which is translated as "wrongdoings" in RSV, is *'alilot* that means simply "doings, actions, deeds." However the connotation of "wrongness" is called for by the participial noun *noqem* whose meaning is "exacter, avenger" and that is rendered as *ekdikōn* in LXX, which is the action of a judge; this is precisely how God is depicted in Psalm 99: "The Lord reigns; let the peoples tremble! He sits enthroned upon the cherubim; let the earth quake! ... Mighty King, lover of justice, thou hast established equity; thou hast executed justice and righteousness in Jacob." (vv.1, 4)

unflinching whenever the doings of the people would contravene his testimonies and statutes, which is precisely the basic tenor of Jeremiah 7. It is obvious then that the mention of Moses and Samuel in 15:1 goes hand in hand with what we found in our discussion of *musar*: the entire matter boils down to following to a T God's "will" scripturalized in the Law, the Prophets, and the Writings, if one is to ensure his "good will."[15]

The appeal to Moses, that is to say, the divine *musar* expressed in the Law, is meant to be a final invitation to the hearers to "return" to God. This is reflected on the structural level of the book. Jeremiah 15 functions as the closing chapter of the first part of the book which is comprised of three "comings" of the Lord's word to the prophet (2:1; 7:1; 11:1). Two features of the text confirm this. On the one hand, to Jeremiah's complaint at the end of chapter 15 (vv.10-18) the Lord replies in a vocabulary reminiscent of his reply to the equally complaining prophet in chapter 1:

> "Be not afraid of them, for I am with you to deliver you, says the Lord." Then the Lord put forth his hand and touched my mouth; and the Lord said to me, "Behold, I have put my words in your mouth ... And I, behold, I make you this day a fortified city, an iron pillar, and bronze walls, against the whole land, against the kings of Judah, its princes, its priests, and the people of the land. They will fight against you; but they shall not prevail against you, for I am with you, says the Lord, to deliver you." (1:8-9; 18-19)

Therefore thus says the Lord: "If you return, I will restore you, and you shall stand before me. If you utter what is precious, and not what is worthless, you shall be as my mouth. They shall turn to you, but you shall not turn to them. And I will make you to

---

[15] Pun intended.

The Covenant of the Lord

this people a fortified wall of bronze; they will fight against you, but they shall not prevail over you, for I am with you to save you and deliver you, says the Lord. I will deliver you out of the hand of the wicked, and redeem you from the grasp of the ruthless." (15:19-21)

On the other hand, a keen ear of the original Hebrew will have detected a pattern that subordinates the second and third instances of the "coming" of the divine word to the first one:

wayhi debar-yahweh 'elay le'mor (And the word of the Lord came to me saying; 2:1)

haddabar 'ašer hayah 'el-yirmeyahu me'et yahweh le'mor (The word of the Lord that came to Jeremiah from the part of the Lord saying; 7:1; 11:1)

The intentionality of such a pattern is evident in its repetition beyond chapter 15 where it delineates the second part of the book (chs.16-23):

wayhi debar-yahweh 'elay le'mor (And the word of the Lord came to me saying; 16:1)

haddabar 'ašer hayah 'el-yirmeyahu me'et yahweh le'mor (The word of the Lord that came to Jeremiah from the part of the Lord saying; 18:1; 21:1)

In turn, the following part of the book opens up with the phrase:

wayhi debar-yahweh 'elay le'mor (And the word of the Lord came to me saying; 24:4)

The Inclusion of the Nations on the Same Footing as Israel

Given the oneness of the tripartite scripture—Law, Prophets, and Writings—and that the Book of Jeremiah functions as an anchor to that oneness, and given that the Latter Prophets as well as the Writings clearly reflect the interest in sharing the teaching of the Law with the nations[16] under the post-exilic new covenant, one would expect to hear a reflection of this concern at the end of the first section of Jeremiah (chs.2-15). After the reference to the punishment into exile as well as the reason behind it (11:1-12:6), we hear the following lengthy passage regarding the post-exilic restoration:

> "I have forsaken my house, I have abandoned my heritage (*naḥalah*); I have given the beloved of my soul into the hands of her enemies. My heritage (*naḥalah*) has become to me like a lion in the forest, she has lifted up her voice against me; therefore I hate her. Is my heritage (*naḥalah*) to me like a speckled bird of prey? Are the birds of prey against her round about? Go, assemble all the wild beasts; bring them to devour. Many shepherds have destroyed my vineyard, they have trampled down my portion (*ḥelqah*), they have made my pleasant portion (*ḥelqah*) a desolate wilderness. They have made it a desolation; desolate, it mourns to me. The whole land (*'ereṣ*) is made desolate, but no man lays it to heart. Upon all the bare heights in the desert destroyers have come; for the sword of the Lord devours from one end of the land to the other; no flesh has peace. They have sown wheat and have reaped thorns, they have tired themselves out but profit nothing. They shall be ashamed of their harvests because of the fierce anger of the Lord." Thus says the Lord concerning all my evil neighbors

---

[16] See especially Is 42:1-7 and 49:5-7; see also my discussion of the Writings in *OTI₃* 129-59.

who touch the heritage (*naḥalah*) which I have given my people Israel to inherit (*hinḥil*): "Behold, I will *pluck* them up from their land (*'adamah*; ground), and I will *pluck* up the house of Judah from among them. And after I have *plucked* them up, I will again have compassion (*riḥam*) on them, and I will bring them again each to his heritage (*naḥalah*) and each to his land (*'ereṣ*). And it shall come to pass, if they will diligently learn the ways of my people, to swear by my name, 'As the Lord lives,' even as they taught my people to swear by Baal, then they shall be *built* up in the midst of my people. But if any nation will not listen, then I will utterly *pluck* it up and *destroy* it, says the Lord." (12:7-17)

The total and impartial equality in the handling of the fate of Israel with that of the nations is evident in several striking features of this passage. First and foremost, we encounter the first instance of the pairs of verbs used to describe Jeremiah's mission in 1:10 ("to *pluck up* and to break down, to *destroy* and to overthrow, to *build* and to plant") appearing together. It is worth noting at this juncture that Jeremiah is the only prophetic book that describes the prophet's mission not so much against Israel or Judah as against "nations and kingdoms," among which Judah is included. This is clear from 1:11-19 where the first instance of the divine punishment is directed against Judah. This is confirmed in 12:7:17 where the nations are handled fully on par with Judah in that their land (*'ereṣ*; earth) is referred to as *naḥalah* (heritage, inheritance) as well as *'adamah*, a "ground" sustaining any *'adam* (human being), just as is the earth of Judah.[17] Equating Judah or Israel with the nations when it comes to God's judgment, which includes his mercy, is not exclusive to

---

[17] See also chapter 25 where "Jerusalem and the cities of Judah, its kings and princes" (v.18) stands at the beginning of the list of nations (v.19-26) introduced in v.13: "I will bring upon that land all the words which I have uttered against it, everything written in this book, which Jeremiah prophesied against *all the nations*."

Jeremiah. It is also found in Amos and Ezekiel. In Amos, at the height of the divine invective against Israel we hear: "Woe to those who are at ease in Zion, and to those who feel secure on the mountain of Samaria, the notable men of *the first of the nations*, to whom the house of Israel come!" (6:1) More emphatically, in Ezekiel, the children of Israel are addressed outright as "nations of rebels" (2:3).[18] In Isaiah, the leaders of Jerusalem are called "rulers of Sodom" and its citizens "people of Gomorrah" (1:10). In Jeremiah, the reason given for viewing Israel with the nations is that both are following Baal instead of God (11:13, 17; 12:16). God's ultimate aim behind scattering the recalcitrant people of Israel among the nations is to have compassion on both and to gather both in his *'adamah* as *naḥalah*.[19] This topic is so central for Jeremiah that it will be revisited in 16:14-21.

---

[18] RSV has "a nation of rebels"; see my comments in *C-Ezek* 69-70.
[19] This is precisely what Paul fully captured: "Just as you [Gentiles] were once disobedient to God but now have received mercy because of their disobedience, so they [Jews] have now been disobedient in order that by the mercy shown to you they also may receive mercy. For God has consigned all men to disobedience, that he may have mercy upon all" (Rom 11:30-32); "But the scripture consigned all things to sin, that what was promised to faith in Jesus Christ might be given to those who believe." (Gal 3:22) In the latter quotation, "all things" means both Jews and Gentiles as I argued in *Gal* 156-9.

Chapter 5
Continued Disobedience to the Law

Now that it has been firmly established that Jeremiah is God's mouthpiece, just as Moses was, the next section (chs.16-23) details how the people mistreated Jeremiah, just as Israel mistreated Moses both in Egypt and in the wilderness, thus revealing their continued recalcitrant stubbornness and demonstrating that their punishment was just and well deserved. This punishment will be the topic of chapters 24 and 25.

The content of chapters 16-17 is controlled by the "coming" of the Lord's word to Jeremiah (16:1-4), in which he is assigned to behave as a "sign" for his compatriots who are to be "without future":[1]

> The word of the Lord came to me: "You shall not take a wife, nor shall you have sons or daughters in this place. For thus says the Lord concerning the sons and daughters who are born in this place, and concerning the mothers who bore them and the fathers who begot them in this land: They shall die of deadly diseases. They shall not be lamented, nor shall they be buried; they shall be as dung on the surface of the ground. They shall perish by the sword and by famine, and their dead bodies shall be food for the birds of the air and for the beasts of the earth."

The reason for this severe punishment is their disobedience to the Law mirroring the behavior of their forebears:

> ... because your fathers have forsaken me, says the Lord, and have gone after other gods and have served and worshiped them, and have forsaken me and have not kept my law, and because you have

---

[1] Compare with Hos 1 and 3; Ezek 24:15-24.

done worse than your fathers, for behold, every one of you follows his stubborn evil will, refusing to listen to me. (vv.11-12)[2]

One would have expected at this point to hear vv.16-18, which describe the Babylonian invasion of Judah. However, those verses are preceded with the promise of restoration beyond the punishment of exile:

> Therefore, behold, the days are coming, says the Lord, when it shall no longer be said, "As the Lord lives who brought up the people of Israel out of the land (*'ereṣ*; earth) of Egypt," but "As the Lord lives who brought up the people of Israel out of the north country (*'ereṣ*; earth) and out of all the countries (*'araṣot*; earths) where he had driven them." For I will bring them back to their own[3] land (*'adamah*; ground) which I gave to their fathers. (vv.14-15)

What compounds the incongruity of the matter is that these verses are introduced with the conjunction "therefore" (*laken*), which would seem more appropriate at the beginning of v.16. Moreover, the promise occurs again almost verbatim in chapter 23 following a passage announcing the new leader of God's restored people (vv.1-6) and thus in a befitting context:

> Therefore, behold, the days are coming, says the Lord, when men shall no longer say, "As the Lord lives who brought up the people of Israel out of the land (*'ereṣ*; earth) of Egypt," but "As the Lord lives who brought up and led the descendants (*zera'*; progeny) of the house of Israel out of the north country (*'ereṣ*; earth) and out of all the countries (*'araṣot*; earths) where he had driven them."

---

[2] Compare with Ezek 2:3-4a (Son of man, I send you to the people of Israel, to a nation of rebels, who have rebelled against me; they and their fathers have transgressed against me to this very day. The people also are impudent and stubborn).

[3] Not in the original.

Then they shall dwell in their own[4] land (*'adamah*; ground). (23:7-8)

So the answer to this apparent conundrum lies in the function of the seemingly misplaced addition of 16:14-15.

The two quoted texts (16:14-15 and 23:7-8) referring to the same promise are found at the beginning and end of this section of the book (chs.16-23) and thus bracket that section. The slight variation in the wording is probably intended to reflect a movement from one situation to another. The first and immediately striking difference is that in the first passage (16:14-15), the recipients of both divine favors, the exodus from Egypt and the exodus from Babylon, are the same: the people of Israel.[5] In the second passage (23:7-8), while the recipients of the first favor are still "the people of Israel," the beneficiaries of the latter favor are "the descendants (*zera'*; progeny) of the house of Israel (*bet yiśra'el*)." Since, in Jeremiah, "the house of Israel" refers to the prophet's contemporaries,[6] then those in exile will never return, but die in the land of their exile. Only their "progeny" born in exile will return. This fully corresponds to what happened in Egypt. All those who were brought out of Egypt were born there:

> These are the names of the sons of Israel who came to Egypt with Jacob, each with his household: Reuben, Simeon, Levi, and Judah, Issachar, Zebulun, and Benjamin, Dan and Naphtali, Gad and Asher. All the offspring (*nepheš yoṣe'e yerek*; souls that came out of the loins) of Jacob were seventy persons; Joseph was already in Egypt. Then Joseph died, and all his brothers, *and all that generation*. But the descendants (*bene*; children) of Israel were

---

[4] Not in the original.
[5] Actually "the children of Israel" (*bene yiśra'el*).
[6] Jer 2:4; 3:20; 5:15; 10:1; 18:6.

fruitful and increased greatly; they multiplied and grew exceedingly strong; so that the land was filled with them. (Ex 1:1-7)

This is confirmed by what Jeremiah tells the exiles in his letter to them (29:1), reflecting their lengthy stay in Babylon:

> Thus says the Lord of hosts, the God of Israel, to all the exiles whom I have sent into exile from Jerusalem to Babylon: Build houses and live in them; plant gardens and eat their produce. Take wives and have sons and daughters; take wives for your sons, and give your daughters in marriage, that they may bear sons and daughters; multiply there, and do not decrease. But seek the welfare of the city where I have sent you into exile, and pray to the Lord on its behalf, for in its welfare you will find your welfare. (vv.4-7)

It is interesting to note that Jeremiah's admonition corresponds to what Joseph did in Egypt: he married "Asenath, the daughter of Potiphera priest of On" (Gen 41:50) and sought—actually secured—the welfare of Egypt (47:13-26). This positive interest in the nations is corroborated in the description of the punishment of Judah in Jeremiah 16:16-18. These verses are unexpectedly preceded by the promise of salvation (vv.14-15) and immediately followed by the equally seemingly unexpected reference to the repentance of the nations:

> O Lord, my strength and my stronghold, my refuge in the day of trouble, to thee shall the nations come from the ends of the earth and say: "Our fathers have inherited nought but lies, worthless things in which there is no profit. Can man make for himself gods? Such are no gods!" "Therefore, behold, I will make them know, this once I will make them know my power and my might, and they shall know that my name is the Lord." (Jer 16:19-21)

Continued Disobedience to the Law

Although the overall message here rejoins what was said earlier in 12:14-17 concerning the inclusion of the nations in the final divine act of salvation,[7] still the reference to the return from exile (16:14-15) before the mention of the exile (vv.16-18) only to end with the post-exilic inclusion of the nations (vv.19-21) is strange and needs justification.

Judah's punishment of exile is described in the following terms:

> Behold, I am sending for many fishers, says the Lord, and they shall catch them; and afterwards I will send for many hunters, and they shall hunt them from every mountain and every hill, and out of the clefts of the rocks. For my eyes are upon all their ways; they are not hid from me, nor is their iniquity concealed from my eyes. And I will doubly recompense their iniquity and their sin, because they have polluted my land (*'ereṣ*; earth) with the carcasses of their detestable idols (*šiqquṣim*; plural of *šiqquṣ*),[8] and have filled my inheritance (*naḥalah*) with their abominations (*to'abot*; plural of *to'ebah*). (vv.16-18)

The only other instance in Jeremiah where *'ereṣ* (earth) as well as *naḥalah* (inheritance; heritage) appear in conjunction with *to'ebah* (abomination) occurs in 2:7 in a context that refers to the exodus from Egypt and the gift of the earth of Canaan as inheritance:[9]

> They did not say, "Where is the Lord who brought us up from the land of Egypt, who led us in the wilderness, in a land of deserts and pits, in a land of drought and deep darkness, in a land that

---

[7] See my comments earlier.
[8] Usually used in the plural form. Out of the twelve instances in scripture, the singular occurs only in Dan 12:11; earlier in 9:27 Daniel has the plural.
[9] See my comments in *C-Josh* 44-51.

none passes through, where no man dwells?" And I brought you into a plentiful land to enjoy its fruits and its good things. But when you came in you defiled my land (*'ereṣ*; earth), and made my heritage (*naḥalah*) an abomination (*to'ebah*). (2:6-7)

An overview of the use of *to'abot* (abominations) and *šiqquṣim* (idols) will readily show that they refer to the worship of other deities in express contravention of God's law. This is clear in Jeremiah and corroborated by Ezekiel:

> For the sons of Judah have done evil in my sight, says the Lord; they have set their abominations (*šiqquṣim*) in the house which is called by my name, to defile it. And they have built the high place of Topheth, which is in the valley of the son of Hinnom, to burn their sons and their daughters in the fire; which I did not command, nor did it come into my mind. (Jer 7:30-31)

> I have seen your abominations (*šiqquṣim*), your adulteries and neighings, your lewd harlotries (*zenut*),[10] on the hills in the field. (13:27)

> They set up their abominations (*šiqquṣim*) in the house which is called by my name, to defile it. They built the high places of Baal in the valley of the son of Hinnom, to offer up their sons and daughters to Molech, though I did not command them, nor did it enter into my mind, that they should do this abomination, to cause Judah to sin. (32:34-35)

> Wherefore, as I live, says the Lord God, surely, because you have defiled my sanctuary with all your detestable things (*šiqquṣim*) and with all your abominations (*to'abot*), therefore I will cut you down; my eye will not spare, and I will have no pity. (Ezek 5:11)

---

[10] From the root *zanah* (commit harlotry).

Their beautiful ornament they used for vainglory, and they made their abominable images (*to'abot*) and their detestable things (*šiqquṣim*) of it; therefore I will make it an unclean thing to them. (7:20)

And I said to them, Cast away the detestable things (*šiqquṣim*) your eyes feast on, every one of you, and do not defile yourselves with the idols of Egypt; I am the Lord your God. But they rebelled against me and would not listen to me; they did not every man cast away the detestable things (*šiqquṣim*) their eyes feasted on, nor did they forsake the idols of Egypt … Wherefore say to the house of Israel, Thus says the Lord God: Will you defile yourselves after the manner of your fathers and go astray (*zonim*; commit harlotry)[11] after their detestable things (*šiqquṣim*)? (20:7-8, 30)

The reason for punishment into exile out of God's land (*'ereṣ*; earth), *inasmuch as it is* his heritage (*naḥalah*), is that the Judahites defiled that heritage through their harlotry with idols (Jer 16:16-18). In order for us to figure the function of the apparently "misplaced addition" in vv.14-15, we need to understand what makes a given "earth" where humans reside not their own property, but God's "inheritance" or "heritage" and ultimately *his* "earth."

Possession reflects personal ownership of property. Students of the European Middle Ages are familiar with manors. The manor is the landed property of the knight or lord who had absolute ownership and authority over both it and the residents who enjoyed and lived out of that land but never owned any of it. An inheritance, especially one that is a patrimony, conveys land as a family estate bequeathed by the father to whomever he *chooses*,

---

[11] See previous fn.

while it always remains a *family* estate. In scripture, the sacredness and inalienability of the patrimony is reflected in the story of Naboth's vineyard (1 Kg 21). As its Latin original *patrimonium* indicates, a patrimony is a reminder (forewarning)[12] by the father and, by the same token, a remembrance of him. Consequently, the only person who can manage the patrimony is the heir assigned by that father.[13] Once in charge, the heir becomes the paterfamilias who, in turn, assigns his own heir, or designates the heir according to the directives of the original paterfamilias. Thus the assignment is always the prerogative of the "father," and this is precisely why the family estate remains a *patri*mony. The oneness of the heir in every subsequent generation ensures the preemption of any tension regarding the patrimony, a tension that would be a predicament in the case of multiple heirs. Since a monarch is the "father" of the kingdom's citizens, he is the manager of his family's patrimony, which amounts to his realm. In Semitic languages, this reality is mirrored in the name *melek* by which the monarch is known, the literal meaning of which is owner or proprietor. His realm as well as his status is either *malkut* or *mamlakah* from the same root *mlk*. The similar situation is found in European countries. A king manages a kingdom or a realm, the latter taken from the Latin *regimen* through the French *royaume*, derived from the Latin *rex* (king) and the French *roi* (king). Because the king is the sole proprietor of the realm, his "children" are also his "subjects" just as in the Roman household where the children as well as the slaves are equally members of the paterfamilias' household and are *subject* to his will.

---

[12] The Latin verb *moneo* is still distinguishable in the English "admonish."
[13] Paul refers to this rule in Gal 4:1-2.

The patrimony was essential in preserving the perpetuity of kingdoms through royal dynasties, whether genetically or by adoption. Ancient kingdoms, however, often underwent upheavals that brought about new dynasties. When this happened, the kingdom's main deity, who functioned as its "parent," guaranteed the perpetuity of the patrimony. It was precisely the oneness of that parent that bridged the gap between one dynasty and another; in essence, all monarchs were equally "sons of (their) god" by assignment (see 1 Sam 12:13; 16:8-12; Ps 2:6-8). Even in the most autocratic dynasties, the patrimony was secure because it lay in the good will of the one deity whose parenthood would span decades and centuries. In the truest sense, only the deity was the parent of the citizens, albeit through the agency of the monarch. The deity alone allowed the monarch as well as the people to reside in its realm *as an inheritance*, never as their own property.

Consequently, the deity of each nation is the incontrovertible as well as ultimate authority concerning the fate of the land on which its people reside; the people have no say whatsoever in the matter. This is clearly expressed in the prayer of King Mesha of Moab inscribed on the Moabite Stone, which was discovered in Dhiban in Jordan in 1868:

> I am Mesha, son of Chemosh, king of Moab, the Dibonite. My father ruled over Moab for thirty years, and I became king after my father. And I made this high place for Chemosh in Qarhoh. I built it as a sign of victory, for he saved me from all the kings and let me see my desire on all my enemies. Omri was king of Israel, and he oppressed Moab for a long time, *for Chemosh was angry with his land.* And his son succeeded him and he too said: 'I will oppress Moab.' In my days Chemosh spoke thus, and I looked down on him and on his throne. And it was Israel which perished

for ever, although Omri had taken possession of the whole land of Madeba. And he dwelt in it during his days and half of the days of his son, forty years, but *Chemosh dwelt in it in my days*.[14]

In the invective against the vanity and impotence of the idols, deities of the nations (Jer 10), we hear that the Lord of Israel is the sole deity. Thus as such he is the judge *of all nations*, as much as he is the King of Jerusalem (Is the Lord not in Zion? Is her King not in her? Why have they provoked me to anger with their graven images and with their foreign idols?—8:19b):

> Who would not fear thee, O King of the nations? For this is thy due; for among all the wise ones of the nations and in all their kingdoms there is none like thee. They are both stupid and foolish; the instruction of idols is but wood! Beaten silver is brought from Tarshish, and gold from Uphaz. They are the work of the craftsman and of the hands of the goldsmith; their clothing is violet and purple; they are all the work of skilled men. But the Lord is the true God; he is the living God and the everlasting King. At his wrath the earth quakes, and the nations cannot endure his indignation ... Every man is stupid and without knowledge; every goldsmith is put to shame by his idols; for his images are false, and there is no breath in them. They are worthless, a work of delusion; at the time of their punishment they shall perish. Not like these is he who is the portion (*ḥeleq*) of Jacob, for he is the one who formed all things, and Israel is the tribe of his inheritance (*naḥalah*); the Lord of hosts is his name. (10:8-11, 14-16)

Still, in order to show his universal justice, before he judges the other nations (12:14-17), the Lord begins by implementing his righteous verdict within his own portion and heritage:

---

[14] E. Lipinski, *The Mesha Inscription*, in Walter Bayerlin, *Near Eastern Religious Texts Relating to the Old Testament*, Philadelphia, 1978, pp.238-9.

> I have forsaken my house, I have abandoned my heritage (*naḥalah*); I have given the beloved of my soul into the hands of her enemies. My heritage (*naḥalah*) has become to me like a lion in the forest, she has lifted up her voice against me; therefore I hate her. Is my heritage (*naḥalah*) to me like a speckled bird of prey? Are the birds of prey against her round about? Go, assemble all the wild beasts; bring them to devour. Many shepherds have destroyed my vineyard, they have trampled down my portion (*ḥelqah*), they have made my pleasant portion (*ḥelqah*) a desolate wilderness. (vv.7-10)

On the other hand, if the Lord is the sole functional deity of all nations, then he is the God of all humankind, of every human being (*'adam*). And, if so, then every local "land" (*'ereṣ*; earth) and "heritage" (*naḥalah*) is de facto and to all intents and purposes a general "ground" (*'adamah*), a place for every and any *'adam*, including the *ger* (neighbor, stranger, outsider): "You shall not wrong a stranger (*ger*) or oppress him, for you were strangers (*gerim*) in the land of Egypt" (Ex 22:21); "You shall not oppress a stranger (*ger*); you know the heart of a stranger (*ger*), for you were strangers (*gerim*) in the land of Egypt." (23:9) That is why, just before the announcement of the exile of the Judahites (Jer 16:16-18) and with the view to include the nations at the time of forgiveness and restoration of those same Judahites (vv.19-21; see also 12:14-17), we hear the restoration cast in terms of a return to the "ground" (*'adamah*) that was given to the "fathers":

> Therefore, behold, the days are coming, says the Lord, when it shall no longer be said, "As the Lord lives who brought up the people of Israel out of the land (*'ereṣ*; earth) of Egypt," but "As the Lord lives who brought up the people of Israel out of the north country (*'ereṣ*; earth) and out of all the countries (*'araṣot*; earths)

where he had driven them." For I will bring them back to their own[15] land (*'adamah*; ground) which I gave to their fathers. (16:14-15)

There are several connotations in this particular phraseology:

1. The comparison with the exodus out of Egypt is intended to bring to the hearers' mind the statements of Exodus:

    > You shall not wrong a stranger or oppress him, for you were strangers in the land of Egypt. (22:21)

    > You shall not oppress a stranger; you know the heart of a stranger, for you were strangers in the land of Egypt. (23:9)

2. When they will be brought back to God's heritage, the returnees are to realize that it was granted not to them, but to their fathers and thus an ever reminder that it is a *patri*mony, not a personal possession.

3. This heritage is an *'adamah*, a place for all and every *'adam*. In this sense it is no different than all the *'araṣot* (earths) where they have been scattered.

4. Ultimately, one may question the value of any "return" to the earth of heritage when, on the one hand, the nations will be sharing in it (Jer 16:19) and, on the other hand, there is no guarantee that those who would inherit it at the

---

[15] Not in the original.

> exodus from Babylon would not defile it as their predecessors had done after their exodus from Egypt (2:6-7).

When one adds to this Jeremiah's instruction to the exiles that they settle in Babylon for good (29:4-7), then the hearers of the book are facing an enigma. Its resolution lies in the phraseology of the two passages immediately following the promise of return (16:14-15), one describing the exile, and one dealing with the nations:

> Behold, I am sending for many fishers, says the Lord, and they shall catch them; and afterwards I will send for many hunters, and they shall hunt them from every mountain and every hill, and out of the clefts of the rocks. For my eyes are upon all their ways; they are not hid from me, nor is their iniquity concealed from my eyes. And I will doubly recompense their iniquity and their sin, because they have polluted my land with the carcasses of their detestable idols, and have filled my inheritance with their abominations. (vv.16-18)

> O Lord, my strength and my stronghold, my refuge in the day of trouble, to thee shall the nations come from the ends of the earth and say: "Our fathers have inherited nought but lies, worthless things in which there is no profit. Can man make for himself gods? Such are no gods!" "Therefore, behold, I will make them know, this once I will make them know my power and my might, and they shall know that my name is the Lord." (vv.19-21)

The common denominator between the two passages is the submission to idols rather than to God. In God's heritage, the nations are to relinquish the service of idols, which service is the reason behind the punishment of Jerusalem. And the only way to be able to do that is to acquiesce to the authority of the God of all nations by obeying his absolute will expressed in his law. This understanding, which is controlled by the first coming of the Lord's word in 16:1, is substantiated in chapter 17:

> [1]"The sin of Judah is written with a pen of iron; with a point of diamond it is engraved on the tablet of their heart, and on the horns of their altars, [2]while their children remember their altars and their Asherim, beside every green tree, and on the high hills, [3]on the mountains in the open country. [4]Your wealth and all your treasures I will give for spoil as the price of your sin throughout all your territory. You shall loosen your hand from your heritage which I gave to you, and I will make you serve your enemies in a land which you do not know, for in my anger a fire is kindled which shall burn for ever." [5]Thus says the Lord: "Cursed is the man who trusts in man and makes flesh his arm, whose heart turns away from the Lord. [6]He is like a shrub in the desert, and shall not see any good come. He shall dwell in the parched places of the wilderness, in an uninhabited salt land." [7]Blessed is the man who trusts in the Lord, whose trust is the Lord. [8]He is like a tree planted by water, that sends out its roots by the stream, and does not fear when heat comes, for its leaves remain green, and is not anxious in the year of drought, for it does not cease to bear fruit. [9]The heart is deceitful above all things, and desperately corrupt; who can understand it? [10]I the Lord search the mind and try the heart, to give every man according to his ways, according to the fruit of his doings. [11]Like the partridge that gathers a brood which she did not hatch, so is he who gets riches but not by right; in the midst of his days they will leave him, and at his end he will be a fool. [12]A glorious throne set on high from the beginning is the place of our sanctuary. [13]O Lord, the hope of Israel, all who forsake thee shall be put to shame; those who turn away from thee shall be written in the earth, for they have forsaken the Lord, the fountain of living water.

The passage begins with an iteration of the sin of idolatry (vv.1-4),[16] followed by verses (vv.5-11) stressing confidence in the sole true God, who alone judges the deeds of the human beings (v.10) according of his law. The oblique reference to the Law is detectable in vv.7-8a: "Blessed is the man who trusts in the Lord, whose trust is the Lord. He is like a tree planted by water (*keʿeṣ šatul ʿal mayim*), that sends out its roots by the stream, and does not fear when heat comes, for *its leaves* (*ʿalehu*) *remain green*, and is not anxious in the year of drought, for *it does not cease to bear* (maʿaśot [*make; do*]) *fruit.*" The only other instance of this metaphor in scripture is encountered in Psalm 1 in conjunction with obedience to the Law: "but his delight is in the law of the Lord, and on his law he meditates day and night. He is like a tree planted by streams of water (*keʿeṣ šatul ʿal palge mayim*), that *yields its fruit in its season,* and *its leaf* (*ʿalehu*) *does not wither*. In all that he does (*yaʿaśeh*), he prospers." (vv.2-3)

The following two verses (Jer 17:12-13) that refer to the heavenly temple of the God of all nations bring to the hearers' mind similar terminology used at the start of Jeremiah's message, (2:4-13) which revolved around breaking the Law that was issued at the exodus from Egypt as well as the defilement of God's heritage:

> ⁴Hear the word of the Lord (*debar yahweh*), O house of Jacob, and all the families of the house of Israel. ⁵Thus says the Lord (*koh ʾamar yahweh*): "What wrong did your fathers find in me that they went far from me, and went after worthlessness (*hebel*; vanity), and became worthless? ⁶They did not say, 'Where is the Lord who brought us up from the land of Egypt, who led us in the wilderness, in a land of deserts and pits, in a land of drought and deep darkness, in a land that none passes through, where no man

---

[16] This iteration is understandably omitted by the LXX.

dwells?' ⁷And I brought you into a plentiful land to enjoy its fruits and its good things. But when you came in you defiled my land, and made my heritage an abomination. ⁸The priests did not say, 'Where is the Lord?' Those who handle *the law* did not know me; the rulers transgressed against me; the prophets prophesied by Baal, and went after things that *do not profit (lo' yo'ilu)*. ⁹Therefore I still contend with you, says the Lord, and *with your children's children I will contend.* ¹⁰For cross to the coasts of Cyprus and see, or send to Kedar and examine with care; see if there has been such a thing. ¹¹Has a nation changed its gods, *even though they are no gods (wehemmah lo' elohim)*? But my people have changed their glory *(kabod)* that which *does not profit (lo' yo'il)*. ¹²Be appalled, O heavens, at this, be shocked, be utterly desolate, says the Lord, ¹³for my people have committed two evils: *they have forsaken me, the fountain of living waters*, and hewed out cisterns for themselves, broken cisterns, that can hold no water."

That the author had in mind this earlier passage when writing chapters 16 and 17 is evidenced in the confession on the lips of the repentant nations at the end of chapter 16:

O Lord, my strength and my stronghold, my refuge in the day of trouble, to thee shall the nations come from the ends of the earth and say: "Our fathers have inherited nought but lies, worthless things (*hebel*; vanity) in which *there is no profit ('en mo'il)*. Can man make for himself gods? *Such are no gods (wehemmah lo' elohim)*!" (vv.19-20)

Further evidence is found in the taunt against the indicting "word of the Lord" (*debar yahweh*) that was issued in 2:4 and pronounced by Jeremiah in 17:15: "Behold, they say to me, 'Where is the word of the Lord (*debar yahweh*)? Let it come!'" Reminiscent of chapter 2, the divine reply to that challenge in chapter 17 is phrased thus:

Continued Disobedience to the Law

¹⁹Thus said the Lord (*koh 'amar yahweh*) to me: "Go and stand in the Benjamin Gate, by which the kings of Judah enter and by which they go out, and in all the gates of Jerusalem, ²⁰and say: Hear the word of the Lord (*debar yahweh*), you kings of Judah, and all Judah, and all the inhabitants of Jerusalem, who enter by these gates. ²¹Thus says the Lord (*koh 'amar yahweh*): take heed for the sake of your lives, and do not bear a burden on the sabbath day or bring it in by the gates of Jerusalem. ²²And do not carry a burden out of your houses on the sabbath or do any work, but keep the sabbath day holy, as I commanded your fathers.' ²³Yet they did not listen or incline their ear, but stiffened their neck, that they might not hear and receive instruction. ²⁴'But if you listen to me, says the Lord, and bring in no burden by the gates of this city on the sabbath day, but keep the sabbath day holy and do no work on it, ²⁵then there shall enter by the gates of this city kings who sit on the throne of David, riding in chariots and on horses, they and their princes, the men of Judah and the inhabitants of Jerusalem; and this city shall be inhabited for ever. ²⁶And people shall come from the cities of Judah and the places round about Jerusalem, from the land of Benjamin, from the Shephelah, from the hill country, and from the Negeb, bringing burnt offerings and sacrifices, cereal offerings and frankincense, and bringing thank offerings to the house of the Lord. ²⁷But if you do not listen to me, to keep the sabbath day holy, and not to bear a burden and enter by the gates of Jerusalem on the sabbath day, then I will kindle a fire in its gates, and it shall devour the palaces of Jerusalem and shall not be quenched.'"

With the mention of the sabbath, which is the day when the statutes of the Law were read aloud to the people, the hearer cannot miss the obvious: the implementation of the divine judgment against Jerusalem (17:27) will be done according to the Law which its leaders did not heed (2:8).

However, the passage concerning the sabbath (17:19-27) is much more pivotal to the Book of Jeremiah than at first strikes the ear. The foremost reason lies in that we have here the only instances of the noun "sabbath" in the entire book. Why suddenly the introduction of the sabbath at this juncture? Given that the sabbath is an institution that started with the exile, when in the absence of a temple the synagogues arose,[17] and since the "word of the Lord" about to "come" (v.15) is a word of destruction for Jeremiah's contemporaries in Jerusalem and Judah (16:14-18) as well as a word of hope for the exiles, the passage concerning the sabbath (17:19-27) looks ahead and functions as an anchor for such hope. Indeed, since Judah is about to be destroyed *because* its inhabitants did not abide by the Law, the returnees to that same Judah will not be secure unless they abide by that same Law. However, in the absence of the temple and, by extension, the priest who is the keeper of that Law (18:18),[18] the Law will have to be read aloud to the people at every "holy convocation" (*miqra' qodeš*) on the sabbath day (Lev 23:3). Once this premise is established in his hearers' minds the author is free to present the second and third "comings" of the Lord's word (Jer 18-20; 21-23) as a showdown between Jeremiah and his opponents whereby the prophet's prayer in 17:14-18 is realized:

> Heal me, O Lord, and I shall be healed; save me, and I shall be saved; for thou art my praise. Behold, they say to me, "Where is the word of the Lord? Let it come!" I have not pressed thee to send evil, nor have I desired the day of disaster, thou knowest; that which came out of my lips was before thy face. Be not a terror to me; thou art my refuge in the day of evil. Let those be put to *shame* (*boš*) who persecute me (*rodephay*), but let me not be put to

---

[17] See my detailed discussion in *C-Ezek* 225-57.
[18] See also Ezek 7:26; Hos 4:6; Mal 2:7.

shame (boš); let them *be* dismayed (ḥatat), but let me not be dismayed (ḥatat); bring upon them the day of evil; destroy (šabar, break) them with double destruction (šabar, breaking)!

The vocabulary of these verses resonates in Jeremiah 19-23:

> Then you shall break (šabar) the flask in the sight of the men who go with you, and shall say to them, "Thus says the Lord of hosts: So will I break (šabar) this people and this city, as one breaks (šabar) a potter's vessel, so that it can never be mended." (19:10-11)

> But the Lord is with me as a dread warrior; therefore my persecutors (rodephay) will stumble, they will not overcome me. They will be greatly shamed (boš), for they will not succeed. (20:11)

> Therefore thus says the Lord concerning Jehoiakim the son of Josiah, king of Judah ... Go up to Lebanon, and cry out, and lift up your voice in Bashan; cry from Abarim, for all your lovers are destroyed (šabar) ... The wind shall shepherd all your shepherds, and your lovers shall go into captivity; then you will be ashamed (boš) and confounded because of all your wickedness. (22:18, 20, 22)

As for the sheep of God's flock, like Jeremiah, they will not be dismayed at the restoration:

> "Woe to the shepherds who destroy and scatter the sheep of my pasture!" says the Lord. Therefore thus says the Lord, the God of Israel, concerning the shepherds who care for my people: "You have scattered my flock, and have driven them away, and you have not attended to them. Behold, I will attend to you for your evil doings, says the Lord. Then I will gather the remnant of my flock out of all the countries where I have driven them, and I will bring them back to their fold, and they shall be fruitful and multiply. I

will set shepherds over them who will care for them, and they shall fear no more, nor be dismayed (*ḥatat*), neither shall any be missing, says the Lord." (23:1-4)

As for the new Jerusalem, just as in Ezekiel 34:23-31 and 37:24-28, it will be under the aegis of the "new David" who will rule in justice and righteousness over both houses of Judah and Israel (Ezek 37:15-23):

> Behold, the days are coming, says the Lord, when I will raise up for David a righteous Branch, and he shall reign as king and deal wisely, and shall execute justice and righteousness in the land. In his days Judah will be saved, and Israel will dwell securely. And this is the name by which he will be called: "The Lord is our righteousness." (Jer 23:5-6)

The rule of justice and righteousness will be so perfect that it will be reflected in the name of Jerusalem itself that will be called by the same name as the new David:

> Behold, the days are coming, says the Lord, when I will fulfil the promise I made to the house of Israel and the house of Judah. In those days and at that time I will cause a righteous Branch to spring forth for David; and he shall execute justice and righteousness in the land. In those days Judah will be saved and Jerusalem will dwell securely. And this is the name by which it [the city] will be called: "The Lord is our righteousness." (33:14-16)

Chapter 6
The Wrath of God

Chapters 24 and 25 are clearly linked to chapter 1 by the similar approach that the Lord uses to introduce his message to Jeremiah:

> The Lord showed me this vision: Behold, two baskets of figs placed before the temple of the Lord. One basket had very good figs, like first-ripe figs, but the other basket had very bad figs, so bad that they could not be eaten. And the Lord said to me, "What do you see, Jeremiah?" I said, "Figs, the good figs very good, and the bad figs very bad, so bad that they cannot be eaten." Then the word of the Lord came to me: "Thus says the Lord, the God of Israel: Like these good figs, so I will regard as good the exiles from Judah, whom I have sent away from this place to the land of the Chaldeans. I will set my eyes upon them for good, and I will bring them back to this land. I will build them up, and not tear them down; I will plant them, and not uproot them. I will give them a heart to know that I am the Lord; and they shall be my people and I will be their God, for they shall return to me with their whole heart." (24:1b-7)

> And the word of the Lord came to me, saying, "Jeremiah, what do you see?" And I said, "I see a rod of almond." Then the Lord said to me, "You have seen well, for I am watching over my word to perform it." The word of the Lord came to me a second time, saying, "What do you see?" And I said, "I see a boiling pot, facing away from the north." Then the Lord said to me, "Out of the north evil shall break forth upon all the inhabitants of the land. For lo, I am calling all the tribes of the kingdoms of the north, says the Lord; and they shall come and every one shall set his throne at the entrance of the gates of Jerusalem, against all its walls round about, and against all the cities of Judah. And I will utter my judgments against them, for all their wickedness in

forsaking me; they have burned incense to other gods, and worshiped the works of their own hands." (1:11-16)

These are the only instances of such dialogue in Jeremiah.

In 25:13 we have the first reference to consigning all of God's utterances in "this book" (*hassepher hazzeh*), which is undoubtedly a reference to the prophet's mission delineated in chapter 1. The linkage is all the more striking in that the end of the punishment of Judah referred to in 25:13a and its reversal in 24:6 are rendered with phraseology reminiscent of that found in 1:10:

> I will bring upon that land all the words which I have uttered against it, everything written in this book, which Jeremiah prophesied *against all the nations*. (25:13)

> I will set my eyes upon them for good, and I will bring them back to this land. I will build (*banah*) them up, and not tear them down (*haras*); I will plant them (*nata'*), and not uproot them (*natas*). (24:6)

> Then the Lord put forth his hand and touched my mouth; and the Lord said to me, "Behold, I have put my words in your mouth. See, I have set you this day *over nations* and over kingdoms, to pluck up (*natas*) and to break down, to destroy and to overthrow (*haras*), to build (*banah*) and to plant (*nata'*)." (1:9-10)

In scripture as well as classical literature in general, fullness or totality is expressed by numeral three,[1] or through the tripling of

---

[1] See *NTI*₃ 22-25.

The Wrath of God

words, phrases or verses within a certain text.[2] We see this pattern in Jeremiah. Since chapters 24 and 25, on the one hand, and chapter 1, on the other hand, form a bracket, it is reasonable to presume that chapters 1 through 25 constitute a "book." The message in this book is cast in three sections, cadenced by the phrase "The word of the Lord came to me saying" (2:1; 16:1; 24:4) Although RSV has two different renditions in the latter two cases,[3] in the original Hebrew *wayhi debar-yahweh 'elay le'mor* is the same in all three instances. The message in the first two parts is graphically detailed. The concise recapitulation of the basic theme in the third part is meant to reinforce the impact of the message to the hearers; however, all the major components are revisited:

1. First and foremost, the true return consisting of rebuilding and replanting (24:6) requires that the exiles regain a true heart of obedience. Only then will they, in truth, pertain to God as his people: "I will give them a heart to know that I am the Lord; and they shall be my people and I will be their God, for they shall return to me with their whole heart." (v.7) This reflects the circumcision of the heart which Jeremiah alluded to at the beginning: "Circumcise yourselves to the Lord, remove the foreskin of your hearts, O men of Judah and inhabitants of Jerusalem; lest my wrath go forth like fire, and burn with none to quench it, because of the evil of your doings."

---

[2] I have pointed out this pattern in my discussion of the other scriptural books where I show that repetition denotes underscoring in a text meant to be read aloud and thus heard. See e.g. *C-Ezek* 61, 111, 142, 157, 167, 185, 221-2, 242-3, 251, 301

[3] "The word of the Lord came to me" (16:1) and "Then the word of the Lord came to me" (24:4).

(4:4) It also rejoins what his contemporary Ezekiel insistently underscored: "Therefore say, 'Thus says the Lord God: I will gather you from the peoples, and assemble you out of the countries where you have been scattered, and I will give you the land of Israel.' And when they come there, they will remove from it all its detestable things and all its abominations. And I will give them one heart, and put a new spirit within them; I will take the stony heart out of their flesh and give them a heart of flesh, that they may walk in my statutes and keep my ordinances and obey them; and they shall be my people, and I will be their God. But as for those whose heart goes after their detestable things and their abominations, I will requite their deeds upon their own heads, says the Lord God" (Ezek 11:17-21); "For I will take you from the nations, and gather you from all the countries, and bring you into your own land. I will sprinkle clean water upon you, and you shall be clean from all your uncleannesses, and from all your idols I will cleanse you. A new heart I will give you, and a new spirit I will put within you; and I will take out of your flesh the heart of stone and give you a heart of flesh. And I will put my spirit within you, and cause you to walk in my statutes and be careful to observe my ordinances. You shall dwell in the land which I gave to your fathers; and you shall be my people, and I will be your God." (36:24-28)

2. The earth of Judah to which the exiles will be brought back is referred to as *'adamah*—an open "ground" where any *'adam* (human being) who abides by God's will (Deut 8:3) may reside. Such *'adamah* was granted to the "fathers" and thus functions as an inheritance, not as a possession (Jer 24:10).

3. The restoration will be geared toward the exiles in Babylon. It will not encompass those who either remained in Judah or fled to Egypt (24:8-10),[4] and therefore did not heed the divine summons to settle in Babylon (29:4-7).

4. Babylon was assigned by God himself to be the agent of the outpouring of his wrath against the disobedient Judahites: "Therefore thus says the Lord of hosts: Because you have not obeyed my words, behold, I will send for all the tribes of the north, says the Lord, and for Nebuchadrezzar the king of Babylon, my servant, and I will bring them against this land and its inhabitants, and against all these nations round about; I will utterly destroy them, and make them a horror, a hissing, and an everlasting reproach." (25:8-9)

5. The inclusion of "all these the nations round about" in v.9 is further detailed in vv.13b-18. The central feature of this passage reflects the earlier teaching concerning the Lord being the God of all nations—Judah and Israel being among them, if not "first" (Am 6:1) among

---

[4] See further Jer 42-43 concerning the Judahites in Egypt.

them: "So I took the cup from the Lord's hand, and made all the nations to whom the Lord sent me drink it: Jerusalem and the cities of Judah, its kings and princes, to make them a desolation and a waste, a hissing and a curse, as at this day; ... [then follows a long list of the surrounding nations] ... Then you shall say to them, 'Thus says the Lord of hosts, the God of Israel: Drink, be drunk and vomit, fall and rise no more, because of the sword which I am sending among you.' And if they refuse to accept the cup from your hand to drink, then you shall say to them, 'Thus says the Lord of hosts: You must drink! For behold, *I begin to work evil at the city which is called by my name*, and shall you go unpunished? You shall not go unpunished, for I am summoning a sword against all the inhabitants of the earth, says the Lord of hosts.'" (Jer 25:17, 27-29) This full equality of all nations before God is underscored in the lengthy harangue against the "shepherds" of the nations (vv.30-38), whose pasture (*marʻit*) he will destroy (v.36), thus putting those shepherds on equal footing with the "shepherds" of Israel "who destroy and scatter the sheep (*ṣoʼn*; flock) of my pasture (*marʻit*)" (23:1). Here again, the closeness with Ezekiel's lengthy invective against the shepherds of Israel (ch.34) is secured through the only instance of *marʻit* in that book: "And you are my sheep (*ṣoʼn*; flock), the sheep (*ṣoʼn*; flock) of my pasture (*marʻit*), and I am your God, says the Lord God." (v.31)

The LXX compared to the MT

At this point it is important to note the structure of the LXX compared to that of the MT (Masoretic [Hebrew] Text). The original Jeremiah 25:13 reads: "I will bring upon that land all the words which I have uttered against it, everything written in this book, which Jeremiah prophesied against all the nations." Given the mention of a closure in a "book" of all the previous oracles of Jeremiah and the reference to his prophecies against the nations, the translators of the LXX opted for eliminating v.13b ("which Jeremiah prophesied against all the nations") and at this point inserted chapters 46-51 which contain the oracles against the nations. Consequently, there is a discrepancy in the chapter order between the MT and the LXX, however, both editions have the same number of chapters and the same content. They are joined again in the concluding chapter 52.

Chapter 7
The Fate of the Exiles

Chapters 26-29 contain a series of head-on altercations between Jeremiah and his opponents regarding the fate of the exiles. The leaders of Jerusalem and Judah insistently took the position that their city would not be sacked. Jeremiah's stand is that not only will this happen, but the exile will last for a very long time (29:4-7). His earlier iterations regarding the restoration of the exiles' children (12:14-17; 16:14-15; 23:7-8) will be expanded upon in a message overarching chapters 30-33, which are commonly known as the "Book of Consolation." This scenario is, to say the least, perplexing for the hearers. Indeed, why should they give credence to a man with such an extreme stand against his opponents who are straightforward, in comparison? In order to preempt this dilemma, the author astutely affirms in each of the first two lengthy sections (chs.2-15 and 16-23) of his first "book" (25:13) that Jeremiah is the incontrovertible prophet of God in the Judah of his time. In the first section the author even puts Jeremiah on par with Moses and Samuel (15:1).[1] In the second section, however, he is far more explicit. In chapter 23, precisely after a detailed coverage of the future restoration under a new kind of leadership (vv.1-8), we have a lengthy passage (vv.9-40) entitled *lannebi'im* (To the prophets; v.9a).[2] The forcefulness of this passage lies in its summation of the similar disparate attacks in the first section. It would appear that its intention is to be the last word in the matter before chapters 26-33:

---

[1] See my comments earlier on the function of that verse.
[2] RSV has "Concerning the prophets."

The prophets will become wind; the word is not in them. Thus shall it be done to them! … the prophets prophesy falsely, and the priests rule at their direction; my people love to have it so, but what will you do when the end comes? (5:13, 31)

At that time, says the Lord, the bones of the kings of Judah, the bones of its princes, the bones of the priests, the bones of the prophets, and the bones of the inhabitants of Jerusalem shall be brought out of their tombs; and they shall be spread before the sun and the moon and all the host of heaven, which they have loved and served, which they have gone after, and which they have sought and worshiped; and they shall not be gathered or buried; they shall be as dung on the surface of the ground. Death shall be preferred to life by all the remnant that remains of this evil family in all the places where I have driven them, says the Lord of hosts. (8:1-3)

Then I said: "Ah, Lord God, behold, the prophets say to them, 'You shall not see the sword, nor shall you have famine, but I will give you assured peace in this place.'" And the Lord said to me: "The prophets are prophesying lies in my name; I did not send them, nor did I command them or speak to them. They are prophesying to you a lying vision, worthless divination, and the deceit of their own minds. Therefore thus says the Lord concerning the prophets who prophesy in my name although I did not send them, and who say, 'Sword and famine shall not come on this land': By sword and famine those prophets shall be consumed. And the people to whom they prophesy shall be cast out in the streets of Jerusalem, victims of famine and sword, with none to bury them—them, their wives, their sons, and their daughters. For I will pour out their wickedness upon them." (14:13-16)

It is worthwhile to quote the entire passage against the prophets in chapter 23. I encourage my readers to read it aloud—or better, have someone else read it to them—in order for them to have a real sense of what it sounded like to the original hearers:

⁹Concerning the prophets: My heart is broken within me, all my bones shake; I am like a drunken man, like a man overcome by wine, because of the Lord and because of his holy words. ¹⁰For the land is full of adulterers; because of the curse the land mourns, and the pastures of the wilderness are dried up. Their course is evil, and their might is not right. ¹¹Both prophet and priest are ungodly; even in my house I have found their wickedness, says the Lord. ¹²Therefore their way shall be to them like slippery paths in the darkness, into which they shall be driven and fall; for I will bring evil upon them in the year of their punishment, says the Lord. ¹³In the prophets of Samaria I saw an unsavory thing: they prophesied by Baal and led my people Israel astray. ¹⁴But in the prophets of Jerusalem I have seen a horrible thing: they commit adultery and walk in lies; they strengthen the hands of evildoers, so that no one turns from his wickedness; all of them have become like Sodom to me, and its inhabitants like Gomorrah. ¹⁵Therefore thus says the Lord of hosts concerning the prophets: "Behold, I will feed them with wormwood, and give them poisoned water to drink; for from the prophets of Jerusalem ungodliness has gone forth into all the land." ¹⁶Thus says the Lord of hosts: "Do not listen to the words of the prophets who prophesy to you, filling you with vain hopes; they speak visions of their own minds, not from the mouth of the Lord. ¹⁷They say continually to those who despise the word of the Lord, 'It shall be well with you'; and to every one who stubbornly follows his own heart, they say, 'No evil shall come upon you.'" ¹⁸For who among them has stood in the council of the Lord to perceive and to hear his word, or who has given heed to his word and listened? ¹⁹Behold, the storm of the Lord! Wrath has gone forth, a whirling tempest; it will burst upon the head of the wicked. ²⁰The anger of the Lord will not turn back until he has executed and accomplished the intents of his mind. In the latter days you will understand it clearly. ²¹I did not send the prophets, yet they ran; I did not speak to them, yet they prophesied. ²²But if they had stood in my council, then they would have proclaimed my words to my

people, and they would have turned them from their evil way, and from the evil of their doings. ²³Am I a God at hand, says the Lord, and not a God afar off? ²⁴Can a man hide himself in secret places so that I cannot see him? says the Lord. Do I not fill heaven and earth? says the Lord. ²⁵I have heard what the prophets have said who prophesy lies in my name, saying, 'I have dreamed, I have dreamed!' ²⁶How long shall there be lies in the heart of the prophets who prophesy lies, and who prophesy the deceit of their own heart, ²⁷who think to make my people forget my name by their dreams which they tell one another, even as their fathers forgot my name for Baal? ²⁸Let the prophet who has a dream tell the dream, but let him who has my word speak my word faithfully. What has straw in common with wheat? says the Lord. ²⁹Is not my word like fire, says the Lord, and like a hammer which breaks the rock in pieces? ³⁰Therefore, behold, I am against the prophets, says the Lord, who steal my words from one another. ³¹Behold, I am against the prophets, says the Lord, who use their tongues and say, 'Says the Lord.' ³²Behold, I am against those who prophesy lying dreams, says the Lord, and who tell them and lead my people astray by their lies and their recklessness, when I did not send them or charge them; so they do not profit this people at all, says the Lord. ³³When one of this people, or a prophet, or a priest asks you, 'What is the burden of the Lord?' you shall say to them, 'You are the burden, and I will cast you off, says the Lord.' ³⁴And as for the prophet, priest, or one of the people who says, 'The burden of the Lord,' I will punish that man and his household. ³⁵Thus shall you say, every one to his neighbor and every one to his brother, 'What has the Lord answered?' or 'What has the Lord spoken?' ³⁶But 'the burden of the Lord you shall mention no more, for the burden is every man's own word, and you pervert the words of the living God, the Lord of hosts, our God. ³⁷Thus you shall say to the prophet, 'What has the Lord answered you?' or 'What has the Lord spoken?' ³⁸But if you say, 'The burden of the Lord,' thus says the Lord, 'Because you have said these words, "The burden of the Lord," when I sent to you,

The Fate of the Exiles

saying, "You shall not say, 'The burden of the Lord,' ³⁹therefore, behold, I will surely lift you up and cast you away from my presence, you and the city which I gave to you and your fathers. ⁴⁰And I will bring upon you everlasting reproach and perpetual shame, which shall not be forgotten." (23:9-40)

An interesting feature of this diatribe against Jeremiah's opponents is the use of the Hebrew noun *maśśa'* in vv.33-40, which is translated as "burden" in KJV, JB and RSV. *maśśa'* is from the verb *naśa'* whose meaning is "raise, lift, carry," whence the participle *niśśa'* used to describe the Lord as being "lifted up" on his throne (Is 6:1). However, *maśśa'* clearly has the meaning of "oracle" that one "raises" against someone in the following instances:

> An oracle (LXX *lēmma*; KJV burden) concerning Nineveh (Nah 1:1a)

> The oracle (LXX *lēmma*; KJV burden) of God which Habakkuk the prophet saw. (Hab 1:1)

This connotation is corroborated in the following parallel instances where we have in the original *maśśa' debar yahweh* (LXX *lēmma logou kyriou*; KJV the burden of the word of the Lord), which is rendered verbatim only in Malachi by RSV:

> The word of the Lord is against the land of Hadrach (Zech 9:1)

> The word of the Lord concerning Israel (Zech 12:1)

> The oracle of the word of the Lord to Israel by Malachi (Mal 1:1)

The clearest instance where the noun *maśśa'* occurs as a complement of the verb *naśa'* is found in 2 Kings:

> And Jehu drew his bow with his full strength, and shot Joram [King of Israel] between the shoulders, so that the arrow pierced

his heart, and he sank in his chariot. Jehu said to Bidkar his aide, "Take him up (*nasa'*), and cast him on the plot of ground belonging to Naboth the Jezreelite; for remember, when you and I rode side by side behind Ahab his father, how the Lord uttered (*nasa'*) this oracle (*maśśa'*) against him: 'As surely as I saw yesterday the blood of Naboth and the blood of his sons—says the Lord —I will requite you on this plot of ground.' Now therefore take him up (*nasa'*) and cast him on the plot of ground, in accordance with the word of the Lord (*debar yahweh*)." (9:24-26)

It is evident in Jeremiah 23:33-40 that the author intended word play on *maśśa'* in order that the message (*maśśa'*) of God through Jeremiah be perceived as a burden (*maśśa'*) by the other prophets. This was because the prophets were deceiving the people by giving their own message to them while insisting that it came from the Lord:

> Therefore, behold, I am against the prophets, says the Lord, who steal my words from one another. Behold, I am against the prophets, says the Lord, who use their tongues and say, 'Says the Lord.' Behold, I am against those who prophesy lying dreams, says the Lord, and who tell them and lead my people astray by their lies and their recklessness, when I did not send them or charge them; so they do not profit this people at all, says the Lord. When one of this people, or a prophet, or a priest asks you, 'What is the burden (*maśśa'*) of the Lord?' you shall say to them, 'You are the burden (*maśśa'*), and I will cast you off, says the Lord.' And as for the prophet, priest, or one of the people who says, 'The burden (*maśśa'*) of the Lord,' I will punish that man and his household. (vv.30-34)

To render the Hebrew *maśśa'* in all three instances, the Septuagint (LXX), by far the most intelligent translation, used the noun *lēmma* that is from the verb *lambanō* meaning "receive, take," which is at the receiving end of the action signified by the

The Fate of the Exiles

verb *nasa'*. The meaning of *nasa'* is "raise, hold over, stretch out" something—including an instruction—with the intention, at times, to "offer, give" that something—including an instruction—to someone. A close parallel in English would be the use of the verb "hold." While "holding" something to give out, one might say to the receiving person, "Hold this." Another example is the phrase "hold a lecture," which obviously would be for others to hear.

Showdown between Jeremiah and the other prophets

Chapters 26-29 build up the vindication of Jeremiah as the only true prophet in the hearers' minds so that the validity of his message will linger even among the exiles. Chapter 26 starts with a succinct recapitulation of the message against the temple which was detailed in chapter 7:

> In the beginning of the reign of Jehoiakim the son of Josiah, king of Judah, this word came from the Lord, "Thus says the Lord: Stand in the court of the Lord's house, and speak to all the cities of Judah which come to worship in the house of the Lord all the words that I command you to speak to them; do not hold back a word. It may be they will listen, and every one turn from his evil way, that I may repent of the evil which I intend to do to them because of their evil doings. You shall say to them, 'Thus says the Lord: If you will not listen to me, to walk in my law which I have set before you, and to heed the words of my servants the prophets whom I send to you urgently, though you have not heeded, then I will make this house like Shiloh, and I will make this city a curse for all the nations of the earth.'" (26:1-6)

The rest of the chapter describes in detail the behavior of Jeremiah's opponents (vv.7-15) and ends with his vindication (vv.16-24). Notice that although "the priests and the prophets and all the people heard Jeremiah speaking these words in the house of the Lord" (v.7), it is specifically the prophets, along with the priests, who are spearheading the opposition and even pushing for a sentence of death (v.11). Yet "the princes and all the people" to whom Jeremiah presents his case (vv.12-15) speak in his defense (v.16). Then, and unexpectedly, we hear some of the elders of the people appealing to a previous prophet to validate the authenticity of Jeremiah's message:

> Then the princes and all the people said to the priests and the prophets, "This man does not deserve the sentence of death, for he has spoken to us in the name of the Lord our God." And certain of the elders of the land arose and spoke to all the assembled people, saying, "Micah of Moresheth prophesied in the days of Hezekiah king of Judah, and said to all the people of Judah: 'Thus says the Lord of hosts, Zion shall be plowed as a field; Jerusalem shall become a heap of ruins, and the mountain of the house a wooded height.'[3] Did Hezekiah king of Judah and all Judah put him to death? Did he not fear the Lord and entreat the favor of the Lord, and did not the Lord repent of the evil which he had pronounced against them? But we are about to bring great evil upon ourselves." (vv.16-19)

Such is a unique instance in the Latter Prophets and thus worth investigating.

Micah the Morashite

The appellation "Micah of Moresheth" occurs only here and in Micah 1:1. The original Hebrew for "of Moresheth" is the adjective "the Morashite," which was kept by KJV. RSV and JB opted for the noun Moresheth, presumably due to the locality of

---

[3] This is a verbatim quotation from Mic 3:12.

Moresheth-gath referred to later in v.14. However, given that the latter is the only instance in the original Hebrew,[4]—unless we consider Mareshah of v.15 being the same as Moresheth—one should consider at least the possibility that the original *morašti* (Morashite) may well have been intended as word play on the verbal root *yaraš* (inherit). Before engaging in this matter, and for the benefit of those not cognizant of Hebrew, below is the relevant text in RSV, KJV, and LXX for comparison.

RSV

¹The word of the Lord that came to Micah of Moresheth in the days of Jotham, Ahaz, and Hezekiah, kings of Judah, which he saw concerning Samaria and Jerusalem … ⁹For her wound is incurable; and it has come to Judah, it has reached to the gate of my people, to Jerusalem. ¹⁰Tell it not in Gath, weep not at all; in Beth-le-aphrah roll yourselves in the dust. ¹¹Pass on your way, inhabitants of Shaphir, in nakedness and shame; the inhabitants of Zaanan do not come forth; the wailing of Beth-ezel shall take away from you its standing place. ¹²For the inhabitants of Maroth wait anxiously for good, because evil has come down from the Lord to the gate of Jerusalem. ¹³Harness the steeds to the chariots, inhabitants of Lachish; you were the beginning of sin to the daughter of Zion, for in you were found the transgressions of Israel. ¹⁴Therefore you shall give parting gifts to Moresheth-gath; the houses of Achzib shall be a deceitful thing to the kings of Israel. ¹⁵I will again bring a conqueror (*yoreš* [heir] participle of the verb *yaraš* [inherit]) upon you, inhabitants of Mareshah; the glory of Israel shall come to Adullam. ¹⁶Make yourselves bald and cut off your hair, for the children of your delight; make yourselves as bald as the eagle, for they shall go from you into exile.

---

[4] I am not counting Jer 26:18, which is an express quotation from the Book of Micah.

116

JEREMIAH: A COMMENTARY

KJV[5]

¹The word of the Lord that came to Micah *the Morasthite* (*hammorašti*) in the days of Jotham, Ahaz, *and* Hezekiah, kings of Judah, which he saw concerning Samaria and Jerusalem ... ⁹For her wound *is* incurable; for it is come unto Judah; he is come unto the gate of my people, *even* to Jerusalem. ¹⁰Declare ye *it* not at Gath (*gat*), weep ye not at all: in the house of Aphrah (*'aphrah*; from the same root as *'aphar* [dust]) roll thyself in the dust (*'aphar*). ¹¹Pass ye away, thou inhabitant of Saphir (*šaphir*; from the root *šaphar* [to be beautiful, fair]), having thy shame naked: the inhabitant of Zaanan (*ṣa'anan*) came not forth in the mourning of Bethezel (*bet-ha'eṣel* [the house that is next door]); he shall receive of you his standing. ¹²For the inhabitant of Maroth (*marot*) waited carefully for good: but evil came down from the Lord unto the gate of Jerusalem. ¹³O thou inhabitant of Lachish, bind the chariot to the swift beast: she *is* the beginning of the sin to the daughter of Zion: for the transgressions of Israel were found in thee. ¹⁴Therefore shalt thou give presents to Moreshethgath (*morešet gat*): the houses of Achzib (*'akzib*; from the root *kazab* [lie, speak falsely]) *shall be* a lie (*'akzab*; from the root *kazab* [lie]) to the kings of Israel. ¹⁵Yet will I bring an heir (*yoreš*; participle of the verb *yaraš* [inherit]) unto thee, O inhabitant of Mareshah (*marešah*): he shall come unto Adullam the glory of Israel. ¹⁶Make thee bald, and poll thee for thy delicate children; enlarge thy baldness as the eagle; for they are gone into captivity from thee.

LXX[6]

¹And the word of the Lord came to Michaeas the son of Morasthi (*ton tou Morasthi*; *hammorašti*), in the days of Joatham, and Achaz,

---

[5] I am including the original Hebrew.
[6] I am including the original Greek followed by the original Hebrew.

and Ezekias, kings of Juda, concerning what he saw regarding Samaria and Jerusalem ... ⁹For her plague has become grievous; for it has come even to Juda; and has reached to the gate of my people, even to Jerusalem. ¹⁰Ye that are in Geth (*Geth; gat*), exalt not yourselves, and ye *in Akim* (*en Akim*; not in the Hebrew), do not rebuild from [the ruins of] the house in derision: sprinkle dust (*ge* [earth, dirt]; *'aphar*) [in the place of] your laughter. ¹¹The inhabitant of Sennaan (*Sennaan; ṣa'anan*), fairly (*kalōs; šaphir*) inhabiting her cities, came not forth to mourn for the house *next to* (*ekhomenon; ha'eṣel*) her: she shall receive of you the stroke of grief. ¹²Who has begun [to act] for good to her that dwells in sorrow? for calamities have come down from the Lord upon the gates of Jerusalem, ¹³[even] a sound of chariots and horsemen: the inhabitants of Lachis, she is the leader of sin to the daughter of Sion: for in thee were found the transgressions of Israel. ¹⁴Therefore shall he cause men to be sent forth as far as *the inheritance of Geth* (*kloironomias Geth; morešet gat*), [even] vain houses; they are become vanity to the kings of Israel; ¹⁵until they bring the heirs (*kloironomous; yoreš*), O inhabitant of Lachis:⁷ the inheritance (*kloironomia; marešah*) shall reach to Odollam, [even] the glory of the daughter of Israel. ¹⁶Shave thine hair, and make thyself bald for thy delicate children; increase thy widowhood as an eagle; for [thy people] are gone into captivity from thee.

It is immediately obvious that the LXX translators, eminently knowledgeable of Hebrew, were not only aware of the word play but actually rendered it, at least partly, in their text. This being the case, I should like to walk my readers through the original in order to show precisely why the author of Jeremiah introduced the quotation from Micah, by name, and how the wording of that reference fits into the message of Jeremiah 26 as a whole. After all, one is hearing Jeremiah 26, not Micah 1 and 3.

---

[7] Added in the LXX from v.13, in order to accommodate its translating the Hebrew *marešah* (from the root *yaraš* [inherit]) into *kloironomia* (inheritance).

The main message of Jeremiah 26 and chapter 7 as well is that God is both entitled and free to dispense of the earth of Judah as he sees fit. Jeremiah has repeatedly underscored that the earth is a heritage bestowed on Judah and not their personal possession. So, at the beginning of the showdown between him and his opponents, those other self-appointed prophets, an appeal is made to a "canonical" prophet, whose book's first chapter not only revolves around God disinheriting Judah because of its sin of disobedience,[8] but also one whose actual appellation reflects that God can do that since he is the bestower of that heritage. Indeed, the Hebrew *mikah hammorašti*[9] (Micah the Morashite) literally means "Who is like the Lord[10] the granter of inheritance." Still the Hebrew is even more compelling. It plays on the consonantal closeness between the participles of the (fifth) active and (sixth) passive forms of the verb *yaraš* (inherit). So, by using the feminine participle of the (sixth) passive form *morešet* to speak of the place of origin of the prophet Micah, one hears that Micah is from the town *morešet* whose meaning is the inherited "earth" (*'ereṣ*) or "city" (*'ir*) that are both of the feminine grammatical gender in Hebrew. Thus, through his magisterial play on the language, the author is preparing for the rest of Micah 1 where the hearers are bombarded with a series of city names, the same names that are part of the heritage of Judah described in the Book of Joshua:

> And Joshua came at that time, and wiped out the Anakim (LXX *Enakim*) from the hill country, from Hebron, from Debir, from Anab, and from all the hill country of Judah, and from all the hill

---

[8] Which was captured by the LXX translators.
[9] This is the participle of the *hiph'il* verbal form, which connotes causality (the one who makes someone else do the action), of the verb *yaraš* (inherit) and, thus, whose meaning is "one who makes someone else inherit."
[10] *mikah* is a shortened form of *mikayyahu*.

country of Israel; Joshua utterly destroyed them with their cities. There was none of the Anakim (LXX *Enakim*) left in the land of the people of Israel; only in Gaza, in Gath, and in Ashdod, did some remain. So Joshua took the whole land, according to all that the Lord had spoken to Moses; and Joshua gave it for an inheritance to Israel according to their tribal allotments. And the land had rest from war. (11:21-23)

This is the inheritance of the tribe of the people of Judah according to their families. The cities belonging to the tribe of the people of Judah ... Adullam ... Lachish ... Achzib, and Mareshah. (15:20-21a, 35, 39, 44)

That the LXX understood Micah 1 in these terms is corroborated by its insertion, not extant in the Hebrew, of *en Akim* (in Akim) in Micah 1:10, precisely in conjunction with Gath: "Ye that are in Geth (*Geth; gat*), exalt not yourselves, and ye *in Akim* (*en Akim*; not in the Hebrew), do not rebuild from [the ruins of] the house in derision: sprinkle dust (*ge* [earth, dirt]; *'aphar*) [in the place of] your laughter."[11] The only plausible explanation for this oddity is that the Greek *en Akim* (Mic 1:10) is a split of the name of the *Enakim* (Anakim; Hebrew *'anaqim*) which is found twice, and in conjunction with Gath, in Joshua 11:21-23 quoted above.

Besides underscoring the truthfulness of Jeremiah's message, the aim of the reference to Micah is to present Jeremiah in a more impressive light. Micah did not have to endure any adversity. His message was readily endorsed by King Hezekiah (Jer 26:19). Jeremiah, on the other hand, barely escaped the sentence of death (v.24). His fate is all the more impressive in that one of his contemporaries was hounded all the way to

---

[11] This is an English translation of the LXX.

Egypt, fetched out of there, and brought back to "King Jehoiakim, who slew him with the sword and cast his dead body into the burial place of the common people" (vv.20-23). The story is even more forceful for the original hearers, since Jeremiah's contemporary was no less than the consummate prophet. Not only was his name Uriah (*'uriyyahu*; my light is the Lord) son of Shemaiah (*šema'yahu*; the Lord heard [heeded, was attentive to]), but he was from Kiriath-jearim (v.20) where the ark of the covenant, containing the tablets of the divine law, was lodged for twenty years (1 Sam 6:19-7:2).

This small excursus on Micah 1 clearly shows that the Old Testament scripture is a closely-knit literary product that is unitary in its structure. And here again, just as with the case of the divine "law" and "instruction" (*musar*), the Book of Jeremiah proves to be the anchor of the entire Old Testament scripture. This is confirmed by the reference to Jeremiah encountered in Daniel, one of the last books of the Writings (*ketubim*), the third part of that scripture:

> In the first year of Darius the son of Ahasu-erus, by birth a Mede, who became king over the realm of the Chaldeans—in the first year of his reign, I, Daniel, perceived in the books the number of years which, according to the word of the Lord to Jeremiah the prophet, must pass before the end of the desolations of Jerusalem, namely, seventy years. (Dan 9:1-2)

The quotation from Micah in Jeremiah and the mention of Jeremiah in Daniel are the only instances of referencing another prophet in the books of the Latter Prophets and the *ketubim*. This would corroborate that the referential prophet of both the exile and its end is Jeremiah. And since it is the demise of Jerusalem and Judah that occasioned the dilemma around which scripture is woven, it is also interesting to note that the Book of

Jeremiah, together with its companion Ezekiel, stand as a diptych at the center of the entire scripture.[12]

Bearing the Yoke

The symbolic story of Jeremiah bearing a yoke (27:2) is intended to confront the teaching of the other prophets who were taking an opposite stand (vv.10-15), namely, that Jerusalem would not fall totally:

> [10]For it is a lie which they are prophesying to you, with the result that you will be removed far from your land, and I will drive you out, and you will perish. [11]But any nation which will bring its neck under the yoke of the king of Babylon and serve him, I will leave on its own land, to till it and dwell there, says the Lord." [12]To Zedekiah king of Judah I spoke in like manner: "Bring your necks under the yoke of the king of Babylon, and serve him and his people, and live. [13]Why will you and your people die by the sword, by famine, and by pestilence, as the Lord has spoken concerning any nation which will not serve the king of Babylon? [14]Do not listen to the words of the prophets who are saying to you, 'You shall not serve the king of Babylon,' for it is a lie which they are prophesying to you. [15]I have not sent them, says the Lord, but they are prophesying falsely in my name, with the result that I will drive you out and you will perish, you and the prophets who are prophesying to you."

Here again, God's absolute hold on the fate of the earth of Judah is cast in terms of its being his heritage, his patrimony; he, and only he, chooses what to do with it and its inhabitants, including the false prophets whom he did not send (vv.10, 15). Just as at the end of chapter 26, here at the end of chapter 27 Jeremiah

---

[12] I am counting the twelve Minor Prophets as one book, the "Scroll of the Twelve."

remains the sole valid prophet, and his message is one of doom issued by the Lord himself:

> Thus says the Lord: Do not listen to the words of your prophets who are prophesying to you, saying, 'Behold, the vessels of the Lord's house will now shortly be brought back from Babylon,' for it is a lie which they are prophesying to you. Do not listen to them; serve the king of Babylon and live. Why should this city become a desolation? If they are prophets, and if the word of the Lord is with them, then let them intercede with the Lord of hosts, that the vessels which are left in the house of the Lord, in the house of the king of Judah, and in Jerusalem may not go to Babylon. For thus says the Lord of hosts concerning the pillars, the sea, the stands, and the rest of the vessels which are left in this city, which Nebuchadnezzar king of Babylon did not take away, when he took into exile from Jerusalem to Babylon Jeconiah the son of Jehoiakim, king of Judah, and all the nobles of Judah, and Jerusalem—thus says the Lord of hosts, the God of Israel, concerning the vessels which are left in the house of the Lord, in the house of the king of Judah, and in Jerusalem: They shall be carried to Babylon and remain there until the day when I give attention to them, says the Lord. (vv.16-22a)

So the hearers would now be primed to listen to the same Jeremiah when he delivers the Lord's message of hope and restoration (v.22b; see also 29:13b), which will be expounded upon in the Book of Consolation (chs.30-33).

Confrontation with Hananiah

An extensive description of the showdown between Jeremiah and Hananiah is yet another story pertaining to the yoke and corroborating the validity of Jeremiah's message, in spite of its being "against the grain." The special feature of the story lies in the name of "Hananiah the son of Azzur, the prophet from

Gibeon" (28:1). His message of divine gracefulness toward Judah seems to be endorsed by no less than the Lord himself. The Hebrew *hananyah* means "the Lord was graceful," while *'azzur* (passive participle of the verb *'azar* [help]) means "one who is helped, who has the support of someone else." Gibeon was the holy place where the Lord was personally encountered:

> They said to the king, "The man who consumed us and planned to destroy us, so that we should have no place in all the territory of Israel, let seven of his sons be given to us, so that we may hang them up before the Lord at Gibeon on the mountain of the Lord." And the king said, "I will give them." (2 Sam 21:5-6)

> Solomon loved the Lord, walking in the statutes of David his father; only, he sacrificed and burnt incense at the high places. And the king went to Gibeon to sacrifice there, for that was the great high place; Solomon used to offer a thousand burnt offerings upon that altar. At Gibeon the Lord appeared to Solomon in a dream by night; and God said, "Ask what I shall give you." (1 Kg 3:3-5)

> When Solomon had finished building the house of the Lord and the king's house and all that Solomon desired to build, the Lord appeared to Solomon a second time, as he had appeared to him at Gibeon. (1 Kg 9:1-2)

So the hearers would be expecting that Hananiah be the mouthpiece of God against Jeremiah, and yet again they are struck by the unexpected outcome. Hananiah is the one preaching rebellion against the Lord, and he will suffer divine capital punishment as a result, and no less at the command of Jeremiah:

> And Jeremiah the prophet said to the prophet Hananiah, "Listen, Hananiah, the Lord has not sent you, and you have made this

people trust in a lie. Therefore thus says the Lord: 'Behold, I will remove you from the face of the earth. This very year you shall die, because you have uttered rebellion against the Lord.'" In that same year, in the seventh month, the prophet Hananiah died. (Jer 28:15-17)

The hearers could not miss the irony: earlier it was Uriah who had been put to death by an earthly king, Jehoiakim (26:20-23); now it is Hananiah who is consigned to the same fate by the heavenly King, the Lord himself.

The Perennial Validity of Jeremiah's Message

The function of chapter 29 is to underscore the perennial validity of Jeremiah's message beyond the exile. This message was captured in the quintessential words of the Psalmist:

> He [the Lord] established a testimony in Jacob, and appointed a law in Israel, which he commanded our fathers to teach to their children; that the next generation might know them, the children yet unborn, and arise and tell them to their children, so that they should set their hope in God, and not forget the works of God, but keep his commandments; and that they should not be like their fathers, a stubborn and rebellious generation, a generation whose heart was not steadfast, whose spirit was not faithful to God. (Ps 78:5-8)

Unfortunately, the authoritative, if not canonical, value of Jeremiah 29 is eschewed in RSV, JB and even KJV, in that the original Hebrew *sepher* (scroll, book) is systematically rendered as "letter" (vv.1, 3, 25, 29), although the same noun appears as "book" in 25:13 (KJV, RSV, JB) and as "scroll" (RSV) or "roll" (KJV, JB) in all instances in chapter 36. In the Ancient Near

The Fate of the Exiles

East anything written (on a scroll) was official.[13] Hence, whether a one page letter or a book of several "pages," a document had to be "read aloud" to its hearer or hearers as well as "dictated (aloud)" to its writer:

> Then Jeremiah called Baruch the son of Neriah, and Baruch wrote upon a scroll at the dictation of Jeremiah all the words of the Lord which he had spoken to him.
>
> And Jeremiah ordered Baruch, saying, "I am debarred from going to the house of the Lord; so you are to go, and on a fast day in the hearing of all the people in the Lord's house you shall read the words of the Lord from the scroll which you have written at my dictation. You shall read them also in the hearing of all the men of Judah who come out of their cities ... Then all the princes sent Jehudi the son of Nethaniah, son of Shelemiah, son of Cushi, to say to Baruch, "Take in your hand the scroll that you read in the hearing of the people, and come." So Baruch the son of Neriah took the scroll in his hand and came to them. And they said to him, "Sit down and read it." So Baruch read it to them. (36:4-6, 14-15)

In contrast to the three above mentioned translations, the LXX reflects more closely the original Hebrew. It has *biblos* (book) in 29:1 and *biblion* (small book) in v.29.[14] Consequently, the official message of Jeremiah, against all opposing prophets, consigned in a "book" (25:13a), remains valid among the exiles and against their contention that "the Lord has raised up prophets for us in Babylon" (29:15). Jeremiah is the sole prophet in whose mouth the Lord has put his own words on the universal scene, within and without Judah alike:

---

[13] This is not unlike electronic communications of today. Documents do not become official until they are printed out, i.e., "in print."

[14] V.25 is rendered in a much shorter form that completely omits the reference to "letters" (*sepharim*) by Shemaiah of Nehelam.

"Before I formed you in the womb I knew you, and before you were born I consecrated you; I appointed you a prophet to the nations." Then I said, "Ah, Lord God! Behold, I do not know how to speak, for I am only a youth." But the Lord said to me, "Do not say, 'I am only a youth'; for to all to whom I send you you shall go, and whatever I command you you shall speak. Be not afraid of them, for I am with you to deliver you, says the Lord." Then the Lord put forth his hand and touched my mouth; and the Lord said to me, "Behold, I have put my words in your mouth. See, I have set you this day over nations and over kingdoms, to pluck up and to break down, to destroy and to overthrow, to build and to plant." (1:5-10)

The official status of Jeremiah's "book" to the exiles is sealed at the end of chapter 29 where the content of the "books" ("letters" in RSV) sent out by Shemaiah of Nehelam (vv.24-25) are deemed "rebellion against the Lord" (v.32), as was the teaching of Hananiah (28:16), and Shemaiah himself is doomed:

> Send to all the exiles, saying, "Thus says the Lord concerning Shemaiah of Nehelam: Because Shemaiah has prophesied to you when I did not send him, and has made you trust in a lie, therefore thus says the Lord: Behold, I will punish Shemaiah of Nehelam and his descendants; he shall not have any one living among this people to see the good that I will do to my people, says the Lord, for he has talked rebellion against the Lord." (29:31-32)

Here again, the name of the opponent is telling. Although the name sounds positive, as did Hananiah, it is so only in appearance. *šema'yahu hannehelami* (Shemaiah the Nehelamite) is an intended pun: though the Lord has heard (*šama'*) the request concerning his heritage (*nahalah*; the first three letters of *nehelami*), Shemaiah is only dreaming (*halam*; the last three letters of *nehelami*) that the Lord would actually hearken to (*šamaʿ*) his request. This is corroborated in the context of an earlier passage: "For thus says the Lord of hosts, the God of Israel: Do not let your prophets and your diviners who are among you deceive you, and do not listen to (*tišmeʿu* from *šamaʿ*) the [your] dreams (*ḥalomot* from *ḥalam*) which they dream (*maḥlemim* from *ḥalam*), for it is a lie which they are prophesying to you in my name; I did not send them, says the Lord." (vv.8-9). Moreover, that such is not a passing thought is evident from the previous passage against the false prophets:

> Am I a God at hand, says the Lord, and not a God afar off? Can a man hide himself in secret places so that I cannot see him? says the Lord. Do I not fill heaven and earth? says the Lord. I have heard (*šamaʿti*) what the prophets have said who prophesy lies in my name, saying, "I have dreamed (*ḥalamti*), I have dreamed (*ḥalamti*)!" How long shall there be lies in the heart of the prophets who prophesy lies, and who prophesy the deceit of their own heart, who think to make my people forget my name by their dreams (*ḥalomot*) which they tell one another, even as their fathers forgot my name for Baal? Let the prophet who has a dream (*ḥalom*) tell the dream (*ḥalom*), but let him who has my word speak my word faithfully. What has straw in common with wheat? says the Lord. (23:23-28)

Chapter 8
The Book of Consolation

Chapters 30-33 stand in contrast to what is written before as well as after them in that they deal exclusively with the future restoration, and thus are known as "the Book of Consolation." These chapters form a diptych: chapters 30-31 are exclusively words uttered by Jeremiah expressing his assuredness that the eventual restoration will take place; chapters 32-33 are constructed around his symbolic action of purchasing a field for the future, amid the debacle around him, to support his firm confidence in what he is proclaiming. His confidence lay not in any kind of surmising calculation on his part, but rather lay in his trust in the divine words of promise.

There is a series of compelling reasons to consider all four chapters as a literary unit. First and foremost is the confirmation that both the Kingdom of Israel, whose capital was Samaria, and the Kingdom of Judah, whose capital was Jerusalem, are one people in God's eyes. This thought brackets the four chapters:

> For behold, days are coming, says the Lord, when I will restore the fortunes of my people, Israel and Judah, says the Lord. (30:3a)

> Have you not observed what these people are saying, "The Lord has rejected the two families which he chose"? (33:24a)

This concern for both Israel and Judah not only hold these chapters together, but this theme runs as a crimson thread throughout the four chapters (30:4; 31:27, 31; 32:30, 32; 33:7, 14).

Secondly, both parts end with a divine oath and use similar wording in conjunction with the new covenant:

Thus says the Lord, who gives the sun for light by day and the fixed order of the moon and the stars for light by night, who stirs up the sea so that its waves roar— the Lord of hosts is his name: "If this fixed order departs from before me, says the Lord, then shall the descendants of Israel cease from being a nation before me for ever." Thus says the Lord: "If the heavens above can be measured, and the foundations of the earth below can be explored, then I will cast off all the descendants of Israel for all that they have done, says the Lord." (31:35-37)

The word of the Lord came to Jeremiah: "Thus says the Lord: If you can break my covenant with the day and my covenant with the night, so that day and night will not come at their appointed time, then also my covenant with David my servant may be broken, so that he shall not have a son to reign on his throne, and my covenant with the Levitical priests my ministers. As the host of heaven cannot be numbered and the sands of the sea cannot be measured, so I will multiply the descendants of David my servant, and the Levitical priests who minister to me." (33:19-22)

Thirdly and most strikingly is that not only are the words of the Lord in chapters 30 and 31 written in a book (*sepher*; 30:2), but the "deed" of purchase of the field by Jeremiah is consistently referred to in the original as a *sepher* (32:10, 11, 12 [twice], 14 [twice], 16). The intention in doing so is revealed at the end of the chapter where we hear that this action by Jeremiah was meant as a blue print for the returnees from exile to follow: "Fields shall be bought for money, and deeds (*sepher* in the singular) shall be signed and sealed and witnessed, in the land of Benjamin, in the places about Jerusalem, and in the cities of Judah, in the cities of the hill country, in the cities of the Shephelah, and in the cities of the Negeb; for I will restore their fortunes, says the Lord." (v.44) The hearer cannot miss the fact that the returnees will sign a *sepher* and such will be according to the words of the Lord that were also consigned as a *sepher* from the beginning (30:2). In both cases one hears that God's action will consist in his "restoration of fortunes" (*šub 'et-šebut*; 30:2; 32:44).

The Two Families

Since the oneness of the people of Israel and Judah is the topic that holds together the four chapters of the Book of Consolation, it would be worth our while to delve into understanding its importance for Jeremiah's message.

In Isaiah the universality of the one scriptural God entailed his inclusion of the nations as well as Israel in the new Zion, under the aegis of the divine law.[1] We have seen this same concern reflected in the message of Jeremiah, especially in chapters 1, 12 and 16:

> "Before I formed you in the womb I knew you, and before you were born I consecrated you; I appointed you a prophet to the nations." Then I said, "Ah, Lord God! Behold, I do not know how to speak, for I am only a youth." But the Lord said to me, "Do not say, 'I am only a youth'; for to all to whom I send you you shall go, and whatever I command you you shall speak. Be not afraid of them, for I am with you to deliver you, says the Lord." Then the Lord put forth his hand and touched my mouth; and the Lord said to me, "Behold, I have put my words in your mouth. See, I have set you this day over nations and over kingdoms, to pluck up and to break down, to destroy and to overthrow, to build and to plant." (1:5-10)

> Thus says the Lord concerning all my evil neighbors who touch the heritage (*naḥalah*) which I have given my people Israel to

---

[1] Is 42:1-7; 66:18-21.

inherit (*hinḥil*): "Behold, I will *pluck* them up from their land (*'adamah*; ground), and I will *pluck* up the house of Judah from among them. And after I have *plucked* them up, I will again have compassion (*riḥam*) on them, and I will bring them again each to his heritage (*naḥalah*) and each to his land (*'ereṣ*). And it shall come to pass, if they will diligently learn the ways of my people, to swear by my name, 'As the Lord lives,' even as they taught my people to swear by Baal, then they shall be *built* up in the midst of my people. But if any nation will not listen, then I will utterly *pluck* it up and *destroy* it, says the Lord." (12:14-17)

Therefore, behold, the days are coming, says the Lord, when it shall no longer be said, 'As the Lord lives who brought up the people of Israel out of the land (*'ereṣ*; earth) of Egypt,' but 'As the Lord lives who brought up the people of Israel out of the north country (*'ereṣ*; earth) and out of all the countries (*'araṣot*; earths) where he had driven them.' For I will bring them back to their own[2] land (*'adamah*; ground) which I gave to their fathers ... O Lord, my strength and my stronghold, my refuge in the day of trouble, to thee shall the nations come from the ends of the earth and say: "Our fathers have inherited nought but lies, worthless things in which there is no profit. Can man make for himself gods? Such are no gods!" Therefore, behold, I will make them know, this once I will make them know my power and my might, and they shall know that my name is the Lord." (16:14-15, 19-21)

In Isaiah, the stepping stone toward this all-inclusiveness was concern about Israel, the Northern Kingdom that fell to the Assyrians well before Judah's demise at the hand of the Babylonians. God's message of mercy toward the exiled Judahites could not bypass the Israelites. This concern for both kingdoms is well developed in the Book of Ezekiel where we hear twice of the story of the two "sisters" (chs. 16 and 23) whom God rescued

---

[2] Not in the original.

The Book of Consolation

from Egypt and, more so, in unmitigated terms in the second part of chapter 37 where the "two" are made into "one," after which the nations are brought into the picture:

> The word of the Lord came to me: "Son of man, take a stick and write on it, 'For Judah, and the children of Israel associated with him'; then take another stick and write upon it, 'For Joseph (the stick of Ephraim) and all the house of Israel associated with him'; and join them together into one stick, that they may become one in your hand. And when your people say to you, 'Will you not show us what you mean by these?' say to them, Thus says the Lord God: Behold, I am about to take the stick of Joseph (which is in the hand of Ephraim) and the tribes of Israel associated with him; and I will join with it the stick of Judah, and make them one stick, that they may be one in my hand. When the sticks on which you write are in your hand before their eyes, then say to them, Thus says the Lord God: Behold, I will take the people of Israel from the nations among which they have gone, and will gather them from all sides, and bring them to their own land; and I will make them one nation in the land, upon the mountains of Israel; and one king shall be king over them all; and they shall be no longer two nations, and no longer divided into two kingdoms. They shall not defile themselves any more with their idols and their detestable things, or with any of their transgressions; but I will save them from all the backslidings in which they have sinned, and will cleanse them; and they shall be my people, and I will be their God. "My servant David shall be king over them; and they shall all have one shepherd. They shall follow my ordinances and be careful to observe my statutes. They shall dwell in the land where your fathers dwelt that I gave to my servant Jacob; they and their children and their children's children shall dwell there for ever; and David my servant shall be their prince for ever. I will make a covenant of peace with them; it shall be an everlasting covenant with them; and I will bless them and multiply them, and will set my sanctuary in the midst of them for

evermore. My dwelling place shall be with them; and I will be their God, and they shall be my people. Then the nations will know that I the Lord sanctify Israel, when my sanctuary is in the midst of them for evermore." (37:15-28)

The teaching is that since the scriptural God is the universal God, he cannot possibly ignore any of the nations, even when others forget them. He is both the savior and the judge of all—not only of those "presumed" to be his:

> Ah Lord God! It is thou who hast made the heavens and the earth by thy great power and by thy outstretched arm! Nothing is too hard for thee, who showest steadfast love to thousands, but dost requite the guilt of fathers to their children after them, O great and mighty God whose name is the Lord of hosts, great in counsel and mighty in deed; whose eyes are open to all the ways of men (*bene 'adam*; children of man), rewarding every man (*'îš*) according to his ways and according to the fruit of his doings; who hast shown signs and wonders in the land of Egypt, and to this day in Israel and among *all mankind* (man; *'adam*), and hast made thee a name, as at this day. (Jer 32:17-20)

The Priority given to the Kingdom of the North

In order to make the point more pertinent, the prophetic message begins by hitting Israel, which is closest to Judah both geographically and religiously. Factually, it is more challenging to have to share with an immediate neighbor than to do so on a mental and thus utopic level with a faraway "neighbor."[3] This, in turn, explains why in the message of salvation priority is given to the Kingdom of Israel and its capital Samaria over Judah and Jerusalem. The evidence for this is convincing in chapter 31 that

---

[3] Luke followed this lead in the parable of the "Good Samaritan" (10:29-37) and in the story of the "Ten Lepers" (17:11-19).

The Book of Consolation

culminates with the promise of the new covenant compassing both houses of Israel and Judah (v.31). The most striking feature of this chapter is that Judah is totally subsumed into Israel. From the beginning God's people are presented as "all the families of Israel" (v.1). Just as in Hosea (11:1), Israel is loved by God (Jer 31:30). However the addressee in Jeremiah is the "virgin Israel"[4] (v.4a; see also v.21a) and, more specifically, Samaria (vv.5, 6). Also in Amos (6:1), the "chief of the nations" is Israel, his people (Jer 31:7). God's "first-born son" Israel is none other than Ephraim (v.9; see also vv.18, 20) as well as Jacob (vv.7 and 11), both of which are typical appellations of the Northern Kingdom in the Latter Prophets.[5] Since Ephraim is the son of Joseph, Rachel's first-born, it is she that is named in 31:15 as having lost her children, that is, the citizens of Samaria and its kingdom:

> Thus says the Lord: "A voice is heard in Ramah, lamentation and bitter weeping. Rachel is weeping for her children; she refuses to be comforted for her children, because they are not."

Ramah, the city of Samuel (1 Sam 1:19; 2:11), stands as a reminder of the locale where Israel committed its official rebellion against God, its sole King, by asking for an earthly king "to govern us like all the nations" (8:4-5).

It is at this point (Jer 31:22a) that the Lord decides to "create a new thing on the earth," as unheard of in the Ancient Near East as "a woman protecting a man". This same Lord *as the God of Israel* (v.23) shows his true face as "the God of all the families of Israel" (v.1) and invites Judah to join in at the restoration:

---

[4] See also Ezekiel 16 and 23.
[5] For Ephraim see, e.g., Is 7:2-9; 9:9; 11:13; Hos 5:3-14; 7:1. For Jacob see, e.g., Hos 10:11; 12:2; Am 3:12-13; 9:8.

Thus says the Lord of hosts, the God of Israel: "Once more they shall use these words in the land of Judah and in its cities, which I restore their fortunes: 'The Lord bless you, O habitation of righteousness, O holy hill!' And Judah and all its cities shall dwell there together, and with the farmers and those who wander with their flocks. For I will satisfy the weary soul, and every languishing soul I will replenish." (vv.23-25)

Only then are God's people addressed as both "the house of Israel and the house of Judah" to whom the new covenant is promised:

Behold, the days are coming, says the Lord, when I will sow the house of Israel and the house of Judah with the seed of man and the seed of beast ... Behold, the days are coming, says the Lord, when I will make a new covenant with the house of Israel and the house of Judah, not like the covenant which I made with their fathers when I took them by the hand to bring them out of the land of Egypt, my covenant which they broke, though I was their husband, says the Lord. But this is the covenant which I will make with the house of Israel after those days, says the Lord: I will put my law within them, and I will write it upon their hearts; and I will be their God, and they shall be my people. (vv.27, 31-33)

In order to underscore the oneness of the people, which is the result of God's intervention, the one "house of Israel" (v.33)[6] will include both Israel and Judah (vv.15-27); together they shall be the one people "Israel" (v.28).

The Book of the Words of the Lord

It is only fitting that chapters 30-31 be presented as "the book of *all* the words that I [the Lord] have spoken to you" (30:2). They contain in a nutshell the entire message of the Book of Jeremiah,

---

[6] See also Ezekiel 37:11 where the "house of Israel" is raised.

The Book of Consolation

beginning with the punishment of Judah for its sins and culminating with the new Jerusalem that "shall not be uprooted (*nataš*) or overthrown (*haras*) any more for ever" (31:40), which is the reversal of the chastisement announced with the first "words" God put in Jeremiah's mouth:

> Then the Lord put forth his hand and touched my mouth; and the Lord said to me, "Behold, I have put my words in your mouth. See, I have set you this day over nations and over kingdoms, to pluck up (*nataš*) and to break down (*nataṣ*), to destroy (*'abad*) and to overthrow (*haras*), to build and to plant." (1:9-10)

From the beginning, the intent of consolation is evident and announced in no uncertain terms: "For behold, days are coming, says the Lord, when I will restore the fortunes of my people, Israel and Judah, says the Lord, and I will bring them back to the land (Hebrew 'earth') which I gave to their fathers, and they shall take possession of (Hebrew 'inherit') it." (30:3) However, this does not mean the restoration to the original status quo ante of the disobedient dynasty ruled unjustly by the first David.[7] Rather, it is a new situation in which "they (Israel and Judah; v.4) shall serve the Lord their God and David their king, whom I will raise up (*heqim*) for them" (v.9). This is clearly expressed in Ezekiel:

> I myself will be the shepherd of my sheep, and I will make them lie down, says the Lord God ... I will save my flock, they shall no longer be a prey; and I will judge between sheep and sheep. And I will set up (raise up, from the same verb *heqim*) over them one shepherd, my servant David, and he shall feed them: he shall feed them and be their shepherd. And I, the Lord, will be their God,

---

[7] 1 Kg 12:6-15; 15:1-3; 2 Kg 8:16-18, 25-27; 16:1-4; 21:1-9, 19-22.

> and my servant David shall be prince among them; I, the Lord, have spoken. (34:15, 22-24)

The closeness between the two messages is sealed in the following chapter of Jeremiah where the Lord presents himself as a shepherd: "Hear the word of the Lord, O nations, and declare it in the coastlands afar off; say, 'He who scattered Israel will gather him, and will keep him as a shepherd keeps his flock.'" (31:10) The fact that the new situation is not a return to the status quo ante is corroborated in what was announced earlier concerning a "new" David in the setting of a "new" exodus:

> Behold, the days are coming, says the Lord, when I will raise up for **David** a righteous Branch, and he shall reign as king and deal wisely, and shall execute justice and righteousness in the land. In his days Judah will be saved, and Israel will dwell securely. And this is the name by which he will be called: "The Lord is our righteousness." Therefore, behold, the days are coming, says the Lord, when men shall no longer say, "As the Lord lives who brought up the people of Israel out of the land of Egypt," but "As the Lord lives who brought up and led the descendants of the house of Israel out of the north country and out of all the countries where he had driven them." Then they shall dwell in their own land. (Jer 23:5-8)

Still the parallelism between the first exodus and the new one lies in that both are aimed at a covenant whose essential expression is the Law (Jer 31:31-33). This is repeatedly stressed in Ezekiel:

> Therefore say, "Thus says the Lord God: I will gather you from the peoples, and assemble you out of the countries where you have been scattered, and I will give you the land of Israel.' And when they come there, they will remove from it all its detestable things and all its abominations. And I will give them one heart, and put a new spirit within them; I will take the stony heart out of their

The Book of Consolation

flesh and give them a heart of flesh, that they may walk in my statutes and keep my ordinances and obey them; and they shall be my people, and I will be their God. But as for those whose heart goes after their detestable things and their abominations, I will requite their deeds upon their own heads, says the Lord God." (Ezek 11:17-21)

For I will take you from the nations, and gather you from all the countries, and bring you into your own land. I will sprinkle clean water upon you, and you shall be clean from all your uncleannesses, and from all your idols I will cleanse you. A new heart I will give you, and a new spirit I will put within you; and I will take out of your flesh the heart of stone and give you a heart of flesh. And I will put my spirit within you, and cause you to walk in my statutes and be careful to observe my ordinances. You shall dwell in the land which I gave to your fathers; and you shall be my people, and I will be your God. (36:24-28)

The closeness between Ezekiel and Jeremiah can be seen not only in the phrase "And you shall be my people, and I will be your God" (Jer 30:22) and in the writing on the heart (Jer 31:33), but also in the passage concerning the full restoration (vv.27-28). Just before the passage about the new covenant (vv.31-33), we hear: "In those days they shall no longer say: 'The fathers have eaten sour grapes, and the children's teeth are set on edge.' But every one shall die for his own sin; each man who eats sour grapes, his teeth shall be set on edge." (vv.29-30) This metaphor to speak of the individual accountability for one's action is found elsewhere in scripture only in Ezekiel: "What do you mean by repeating this proverb concerning the land of Israel, 'The fathers have eaten sour grapes, and the children's teeth are set on edge'? As I live, says the Lord God, this proverb shall no more be used by you in Israel. Behold, all souls are mine; the soul of the father as well as the soul of the son is mine: the soul that sins shall die." (18:2-4) This explains the pertinent addition regarding the new covenant: "And no longer shall each man teach his neighbor and each his brother, saying, 'Know the Lord,' for they shall all know me, from the least (youngest) of them to the greatest (eldest), says the Lord." (Jer 31:34)

The New Covenant

As is made clear in the above passages from Ezekiel, the new covenant does not entail a "law-less" situation. Consequently the last phrase in Jeremiah 31:34 "for I will forgive their iniquity, and I will remember their sin no more" is not tantamount to a license to do one's own will. Rather one is to do the will of God, as a slave[8] would his master's. This is implied in 30:8-9:

> And it shall come to pass in that day, says the Lord of hosts, that I will break the yoke from off their neck, and I will burst their bonds, and strangers shall no more make *servants* (*ya'abdu*) of them. But they shall *serve* (*'abedu*) the Lord their God and David their king, whom I will raise up for them.

That is why, being unwarranted save for God's goodness, the new covenant is an unexpected second chance. Still, since the phrase "new covenant" in Jeremiah is the only instance of such in the Old Testament, the most relevant question is, "What constitutes the newness of this covenant?" To understand its newness as a mere renewal is unsatisfactory. As is clear from the Book of Exodus, the story of the Mosaic covenant, by which Israel and Judah are bound, is already a renewed covenant:

> And Moses turned, and went down from the mountain with the two tables of the testimony in his hands, tables that were written

---

[8] My readers are reminded that the original Hebrew *'abad* behind the English "serve" has this connotation.

on both sides; on the one side and on the other were they written. And the tables were the work of God, and the writing was the writing of God, graven upon the tables. When Joshua heard the noise of the people as they shouted, he said to Moses, "There is a noise of war in the camp." But he said, "It is not the sound of shouting for victory, or the sound of the cry of defeat, but the sound of singing that I hear." And as soon as he came near the camp and saw the calf and the dancing, Moses' anger burned hot, and he threw the tables out of his hands and broke them at the foot of the mountain ... The Lord said to Moses, "Cut two tables of stone like the first; and I will write upon the tables the words that were on the first tables, which you broke ... So Moses cut two tables of stone like the first; and he rose early in the morning and went up on Mount Sinai, as the Lord had commanded him, and took in his hand two tables of stone ... And he [the Lord] said, "Behold, I make a covenant. Before all your people I will do marvels, such as have not been wrought in all the earth or in any nation; and all the people among whom you are shall see the work of the Lord; for it is a terrible thing that I will do with you." ... And the Lord said to Moses, "Write these words; in accordance with these words I have made a covenant with you and with Israel." And he was there with the Lord forty days and forty nights; he neither ate bread nor drank water. And he wrote upon the tables the words of the covenant, the ten commandments. When Moses came down from Mount Sinai, with the two tables of the testimony in his hand as he came down from the mountain, Moses did not know that the skin of his face shone because he had been talking with God. (Ex 32:15-19; 34:1, 4, 10, 27-29)

So the clue to the element of novelty in the Jeremianic "new covenant" must lie in the divine law being written on one's heart rather than on tablets of stone.[9] The argument becomes more

---

[9] This is not as reassuring as it sounds at first hearing; indeed, if the people break the Law this time round, it is their hearts that will be broken, which is reflective of final judgment.

convincing when one realizes that there is no mention at all of "heart" in Exodus 32-34. On the other hand, we hear of a passage which describes that post-exilic second chance to abide by the Law in terms of a "new heart" and, no less, in opposition to a heart of stone, the latter term being reminiscent of the first covenant:

> Therefore say to the house of Israel, Thus says the Lord God: It is not for your sake, O house of Israel, that I am about to act, but for the sake of my holy name, which you have profaned among the nations to which you came. And I will vindicate the holiness of my great name, which has been profaned among the nations, and which you have profaned among them; and the nations will know that I am the Lord, says the Lord God, when through you I vindicate my holiness before their eyes. For I will take you from the nations, and gather you from all the countries, and bring you into your own land. I will sprinkle clean water upon you, and you shall be clean from all your uncleannesses, and from all your idols I will cleanse you. A new heart I will give you, and a new spirit I will put within you; and I will take out of your flesh the heart of stone and give you a heart of flesh. And I will put my spirit within you, and cause you to walk in my statutes and be careful to observe my ordinances. (Ezek 36:22-27)

Paul understood fully this reality when he wrote: "There is therefore now no condemnation for those who are in Christ Jesus. For *the law of the Spirit of life* in Christ Jesus has set me free from the law of sin and death." (Rom 8:1-2)

Looking ahead

The symbolic story of Jeremiah in chapters 32-33 is phrased in a way that forms a hinge between the message of consolation (chapters 30-31) and the following chapters (34-45). The most obvious link is that Jeremiah's activity in chapters 32-33 and in

The Book of Consolation

chapters 34 and 37-39 takes place during the reign of King Zedekiah. Moreover, the interest in Zedekiah is due to his symbolic name *ṣidqiyyahu* whose meaning is "the righteousness of the Lord" or "the Lord is my righteousness." Just as in the case of the prophet Hananiah, who lived under him (28:1), the name is used ironically since Zedekiah acts in a manner that contravenes God's righteousness. The function of this irony is revealed later in chapter 33 where we hear:

> Behold, the days are coming, says the Lord, when I will fulfil (*haqimoti*; I shall make stand, I shall raise up) the promise (*dabar tob*; good word) I made to the house of Israel and the house of Judah. In those days and at that time I will cause a righteous Branch to spring forth for David; and he shall execute justice and righteousness in the land. In those days Judah will be saved and Jerusalem will dwell securely. And this is the name by which it [the city] will be called: "The Lord is our righteousness (*yahweh ṣidqenu*)." (vv.14-16)

This statement recalls an earlier one:

> Behold, the days are coming, says the Lord, when I will raise up (*haqimoti*) for David a righteous (*ṣaddiq*) Branch, and he shall reign as king and deal wisely, and shall execute justice and righteousness (*ṣedaqah*) in the land. In his days Judah will be saved, and Israel will dwell securely. And this is the name by which he will be called: "The Lord is our righteousness (*yahweh ṣidqenu*)." (23:5-6)

These two passages clearly have in mind not only Zedekiah, but also his brother Jehoiakim (*yehoyaqim*; the Lord shall raise up) who reigned before him and was supposed to be the righteous king "raised up" by God. He ended up, however, betraying God's cause. Jehoiakim will be the reigning monarch of chapters

35-36. These two kings, in total disregard to the words of Jeremiah, rebelled against Nebuchadnezzar of Babylon (2 Kg 24:1b, 19-20b), an action that occasioned the two waves of Judahite exiles to Babylon (24:10-18; 25:8-21).

Opposite these kings we have Jeremiah who is cast as a prototype of hope for his contemporaries or, at least, for their children. In spite of the message he sent to the exiles to "build houses and live in them; plant gardens and eat their produce" (29:5), "take wives and have sons and daughters; take wives for your sons, and give your daughters in marriage, that they may bear sons and daughters; multiply there, and do not decrease" (v.6), and "seek the welfare of the city of their exile" (v.7), Jeremiah himself is summoned by the Lord to buy a field in Anathoth, his hometown (32:6-7), in view of the Lord's later words (Fields shall be bought for money, and deeds (*sepher*, book) shall be signed and sealed and witnessed, in the land of Benjamin, in the places about Jerusalem, and in the cities of Judah, in the cities of the hill country, in the cities of the Shephelah, and in the cities of the Negeb; for I will restore their fortunes; v.44):

> ⁶Jeremiah said, "The word of the Lord came to me: ⁷Behold, Hanamel the son of Shallum your uncle will come to you and say, 'Buy my field which is at Anathoth, for the right of redemption by purchase is yours.' ⁸Then Hanamel my cousin came to me in the court of the guard, in accordance with the word of the Lord, and said to me, 'Buy my field which is at Anathoth in the land of Benjamin, for the right of possession and redemption is yours; buy it for yourself.' Then I knew that this was the word of the Lord. ⁹And I bought the field at Anathoth from Hanamel my cousin, and weighed out the money to him, seventeen shekels of silver. ¹⁰I signed the deed, sealed it, got witnesses, and weighed the money on scales. ¹¹Then I took the sealed deed of purchase, containing

the terms and conditions, and the open copy; ¹²and I gave the deed of purchase to Baruch the son of Neriah son of Mahseiah, in the presence of Hanamel my cousin, in the presence of the witnesses who signed the deed of purchase, and in the presence of all the Jews who were sitting in the court of the guard. ¹³I charged Baruch in their presence, saying, ¹⁴"Thus says the Lord of hosts, the God of Israel: Take these deeds, both this sealed deed of purchase and this open deed, and put them in an earthenware vessel, that they may last for a long time. ¹⁵For thus says the Lord of hosts, the God of Israel: Houses and fields and vineyards shall again be bought in this land.'" (32:6-15)

The story sets not so much Jeremiah himself, but rather the word of the Lord through him, against the kings of Judah, as will be made clear in chapter 36. In and of itself the story is impressive. Still, for the original hearers, it bore an even more compelling message in that the names of all those involved reflect positive connotations pointing to God's ultimate mercy. Jeremiah's uncle's name, Shallum (*šallum*) is from the same root as "peace" (*šalom*).[10] His son's name Hanamel (*ḥanam'el*) whose meaning is God (*'el*) [will grant] "without compensation, undeservedly" (*ḥinnam*). As for Baruch (*baruk*), who will write the "book" of the transaction of the sale and purchase of the field (v.12), his name means "blessed" while his father is Neriah (*neriyyah*; the lamp of the Lord) and his grandfather is Mahseiah (*maḥseyah*; the Lord is a refuge).[11]

---

[10] Actually in Hebrew the consonants of both words are *šlm*. Moreover, in 33:6 the Lord will say: "Behold, I will bring to it health and healing, and I will heal them and reveal to them abundance of prosperity (*šalom*) and security."

[11] See earlier Jeremiah's prayer (17:14-18) in which he says "thou art my refuge (*maḥasi*) in the day of evil" (v.17b).

That this story of Jeremiah's hope is the direct foreshadowing of the "good word"[12] of the Lord in 33:14-16 is readily detectable in the Hebrew and thus understood by the original addressees. Both "uncle," in speaking of Shallum (32:7) and "cousin," in speaking of his son Hanamel (vv.8, 9, 12), are translations of the same original *dod*,[13] whose meaning is "beloved."[14] However, the consonantal Hebrew is more often than not *dwd*, which is systematically vocalized as *dod* except in the case of David (consonantal *dwd*) where it is vocalized as *dawid*.

---

[12] This is the literal translation of the original Hebrew *dabar tob* (Jer 33:14) rendered as "promise" in RSV and as (closer to the original) "good thing" in KJV.

[13] Actually, the Hebrew in vv.8 and 9 is *ben dodi* (my uncle's son).

[14] This is how *dod* is translated throughout the Song of Songs.

Chapter 9
The Demise of the City and the Rise of Scripture

The Sin of Zedekiah

Chapters 34-36 are constructed as a chiasm (ABA') underscoring the disobedient attitude of the kings—Zedekiah in chapter 34 and Jehoiakim in chapter 36—which contrasts with the unflinching obedience of the Rechabites to the will of their forebear (ch.35).

The story concerning Zedekiah paints him as contravening the express command of God. He reneges on the covenant of liberty (*deror*; 34:8, 15, 17 [twice]) for the slaves in the jubilee year:

> And you shall count seven weeks of years, seven times seven years, so that the time of the seven weeks of years shall be to you forty-nine years. Then you shall send abroad the loud trumpet on the tenth day of the seventh month; on the day of atonement you shall send abroad the trumpet throughout all your land. And you shall hallow the fiftieth year, and proclaim liberty (*deror*) throughout the land to all its inhabitants; it shall be a jubilee for you, when each of you shall return to his property and each of you shall return to his family. A jubilee shall that fiftieth year be to you; in it you shall neither sow, nor reap what grows of itself, nor gather the grapes from the undressed vines. For it is a jubilee; it shall be holy to you; you shall eat what it yields out of the field. (Lev 25:8-12)[1]

---

[1] These are the only instances of *deror* in Jeremiah and Leviticus.

Moreover, Jeremiah's criticism of the king's action starts with a reference to the exodus from Egypt and to the similar misbehavior of the king's "fathers":

> The word of the Lord came to Jeremiah from the Lord: "Thus says the Lord, the God of Israel: I made a covenant with your fathers when I brought them out of the land of Egypt, out of the house of bondage (*'abadim*; slaves), saying, 'At the end of six years each of you must set free the fellow Hebrew who has been sold to you and has served you six years; you must set him free from your service.' But your fathers did not listen to me or incline their ears to me. You recently repented and did what was right in my eyes by proclaiming liberty (*deror*), each to his neighbor, and you made a covenant before me in the house which is called by my name; but then you turned around and profaned my name when each of you took back his male and female slaves, whom you had set free according to their desire, and you brought them into subjection to be your slaves (*'abadim*)." (Jer 34:12-16)

It is as though the people had never left Egypt and, consequently, God had not liberated them through the exodus he orchestrated! Such a thought is not as strange as it sounds when one recalls the classic text of Deuteronomy concerning the king's duty:

> When you come to the land which the Lord your God gives you, and you possess it and dwell in it, and then say, "I will set a king over me, like all the nations that are round about me"; you may indeed set as king over you him whom the Lord your God will choose. One from among your brethren you shall set as king over you; you may not put a foreigner over you, who is not your brother. Only he must not multiply horses for himself, or cause the people to return to Egypt in order to multiply horses, since the Lord has said to you, "You shall never return that way again." (17:14-16)

That the author had this thought in mind will become evident later when we hear that Zedekiah asked for help from Egypt against Babylon, in direct contravention of Jeremiah's advice (Jer 37:3-10). In this Zedekiah did not prove to be better than his "father" Solomon who married the daughter of Pharaoh, thus entering into an alliance with Egypt:

> Solomon made a marriage alliance with Pharaoh king of Egypt; he took Pharaoh's daughter, and brought her into the city of David, until he had finished building his own house and the house of the Lord and the wall around Jerusalem ... And Solomon gathered together chariots (*rekeb*) and horsemen; he had fourteen hundred chariots (*rekeb*) and twelve thousand horsemen, whom he stationed in the chariot (*rekeb*) cities and with the king in Jerusalem. And the king made silver as common in Jerusalem as stone, and he made cedar as plentiful as the sycamore of the Shephelah. And Solomon's import of horses was from Egypt and Kue, and the king's traders received them from Kue at a price. A chariot (*merkabah*) could be imported from Egypt for six hundred shekels of silver, and a horse for a hundred and fifty; and so through the king's traders they were exported to all the kings of the Hittites and the kings of Syria. (1 Kg 3:1; 10:26-29)

The Rechabites (Rekabites)

Jeremiah 35 functions as a corrective to the attitude of Jerusalem and its kings by showing the faithfulness of the Rechabites to the commands of their father. It is strategically positioned between chapters 34 and 36, which are critical of Kings Zedekiah and Jehoiakim. Inexplicably, both KJV and RSV opted for "Rechabites" over "Rekabites" as in JB. In so doing they obfuscated the word play between the original *rekabim* (Jer 35:2, 3, 5,18) and their forefather Jonadab the son of Rechab (*ben rekab*; vv.6, 8, 14, 16, 19), on the one hand, and the

Hebrew *rekeb* for chariot, on the other hand. This is corroborated in that the only other instance in scripture where we hear of Jehonadab[2] the son of Rechab is in the story of the extermination of Ahab's royal family at the hand of Jehu, who was anointed by Elisha (2 Kg 9-10), which is, perhaps, the epitome of anti-kingly attitude. Jehonadab appears meteorically, only to disappear after a few verses. He is witness to Jehu's cleansing of Israel from all the vestiges of the worship of Baal which was introduced into Samaria by Ahab, purportedly under the influence of his wife Jezebel (1 Kg 16:29-32), thus making of him the worst king of Israel up to his time (v.33). It would be helpful for me to quote the entire passage in order to show the intended closeness between it and Jeremiah 35:

> [12]Then he set out and went to Samaria. On the way, when he was at Beth-eked of the *Shepherds*, [13]Jehu met the kinsmen of Ahaziah king of Judah, and he said, "Who are you?" And they answered, "We are the kinsmen of Ahaziah, and we came down to visit the royal princes and the sons of the queen mother." [14]He said, "Take them alive." And they took them alive, and slew them at the pit of Beth-eked, forty-two persons, and he spared none of them. [15]And when he departed from there, he met Jehonadab the son of Rechab (*rekab*) coming to meet him; and he greeted him, and said to him, "Is your heart true to my heart as mine is to yours?" And Jehonadab answered, "It is." Jehu said, "If it is, give me your hand." So he gave him his hand. And Jehu took him up with him into the chariot (*merkabah*). [16]And he said, "Come with me, and see my zeal for the Lord." So he had him ride (*yarkib* from the verb *rakab*) in his chariot (*rekeb*). [17]And when he came to Samaria, he slew all that remained to Ahab in Samaria, till he had wiped them out, according to the word of the Lord which he spoke to Elijah. [18]Then Jehu assembled all the people, and said to them,

---

[2] Jonadab is a shortened form of Jehonadab.

"Ahab served Baal a little; but Jehu will serve him much. ¹⁹Now therefore call to me all the prophets of Baal, all his worshipers and all his priests; let none be missing, for I have a great sacrifice to offer to Baal; whoever is missing shall not live." But Jehu did it with cunning in order to destroy the worshipers of Baal. ²⁰And Jehu ordered, "Sanctify a solemn assembly for Baal." So they proclaimed it. ²¹And Jehu sent throughout all Israel; and all the worshipers of Baal came, so that there was not a man left who did not come. And they entered the house of Baal, and the house of Baal was filled from one end to the other. ²²He said to him who was in charge of the wardrobe, "Bring out the vestments for all the worshipers of Baal." So he brought out the vestments for them. ²³Then Jehu went into the house of Baal with Jehonadab the son of Rechab; and he said to the worshipers of Baal, "Search, and see that there is no servant of the Lord here among you, but only the worshipers of Baal." ²⁴Then he went in to offer sacrifices and burnt offerings. Now Jehu had stationed eighty men outside, and said, "The man who allows any of those whom I give into your hands to escape shall forfeit his life." ²⁵So as soon as he had made an end of offering the burnt offering, Jehu said to the guard and to the officers, "Go in and slay them; let not a man escape." So when they put them to the sword, the guard and the officers cast them out and went into the inner room of the house of Baal ²⁶and they brought out the pillar that was in the house of Baal, and burned it. ²⁷And they demolished the pillar of Baal, and demolished the house of Baal, and made it a latrine to this day. (2 Kg 10:12-27)

Two things are worth of note: (1) the name of the locality, Beth-eked of the Shepherds, where Jehu met Jehonadab, and (2) the invitation of Jehu to have Jehonadab ride in his chariot. The mention of both is deliberate. In the first case, the addition of "of the Shepherds" in v.12 is unexpected, considering that the short form of Beth-eked is used in v.14. What is all the more striking is that it is the only instance of "shepherds" in 1 and 2

Kings.³ This stress on shepherds corresponds to what we learned in Jeremiah 35 concerning the descendants of Rechab:

> But they answered, "We will drink no wine, for Jonadab the son of Rechab, our father, commanded us, 'You shall not drink wine, neither you nor your sons for ever; you shall not build a house; you shall not sow seed; you shall not plant or have a vineyard; but you shall live in tents all your days, that you may live many days in the land where you sojourn.' We have obeyed the voice of Jonadab the son of Rechab, our father, in all that he commanded us, to drink no wine all our days, ourselves, our wives, our sons, or our daughters, and not to build houses to dwell in. We have no vineyard or field or seed; but we have lived in tents, and have obeyed and done all that Jonadab our father commanded us. (vv.6-10)⁴

Still, the trained ear of an attentive hearer of scripture would have already detected a link to the life of shepherds in the shorter name of the locality, Beth-eked (*bet 'eqed*). Seven of the ten occurrences of the root *'aqad* (bind) are found in the story describing how Jacob, through cunning, acquired the sheep of his father-in-law Laban (Gen 30:25-31:12).⁵ On the other hand, the connotation "bind" of *'aqad*, as evidenced in Genesis 22:9,⁶ aptly fits the topic of "covenant" between Zedekiah and the people of Jerusalem in Jeremiah 34:

---

³ In 1 Kg 22:17 we have the singular "shepherd": "And he [Micaiah] said, 'I saw all Israel scattered upon the mountains, as sheep that have no shepherd.'"

⁴ Having vineyards and drinking its produce assumes a lengthy time of sedentary residence in one place.

⁵ Gen 30:35, 39, 40; 31:8 [twice], 10, 12. The Hebrew original *'aquddim* is translated as "striped."

⁶ "When they came to the place of which God had told him, Abraham built an altar there, and laid the wood in order, and bound (*wayya'aqod*) Isaac his son, and laid him on the altar, upon the wood."

The word which came to Jeremiah from the Lord, after King Zedekiah had made a covenant with all the people in Jerusalem to make a proclamation of liberty to them, that every one should set free his Hebrew slaves, male and female, so that no one should enslave a Jew, his brother. And they obeyed, all the princes and all the people who had entered into the covenant that every one would set free his slave, male or female, so that they would not be enslaved again; they obeyed and set them free. But afterward they turned around and took back the male and female slaves they had set free, and brought them into subjection as slaves. (vv.8-11)[7]

The cunning of Jacob, Zedekiah's forefather, ended him in the "slavery" of Egypt; the cunning of Zedekiah is about to end him in the "liberty (*deror*) to the sword, to pestilence, and to famine" (v.17): "And the men who transgressed my covenant and did not keep the terms of the covenant which they made before me … I will give them into the hand of their enemies and into the hand of those who seek their lives. Their dead bodies shall be food for the birds of the air and the beasts of the earth." (vv.18, 20)

At the other end of the spectrum, a "shepherd" of the "house of the covenant" (*bet 'eqed*), Jehonadab (Jonadab) the son of Rechab (*rekab*), was chosen to ride (*rakab*) in the chariot of the victorious Jehu, who slew at Beth-eked of the Shepherds the kinsmen of Ahaziah king of Judah (2 Kg 10:13-14), the predecessor of Zedekiah. Jehonadab's descendants were obedient to the "command" of their forbear (Jer 35:14), a mere human being, whereas "the men of Judah and the inhabitants of Jerusalem" (v.13a) did not obey God himself (v.16) and, by so doing, they did not "receive instruction (*musar*) and listen to my words" (v.13b). That is why, before the indictment of Zedekiah

---

[7] Those who know Arabic are familiar with the verb *'aqada* (bind) and the noun *'aqd* (binding agreement; deed).

(ch.34), the promise uttered earlier (ch.33) to the "houses of David and Levi," traditionally the kingly and priestly dynasties respectively, is now bestowed on the "house of the Rechabites":

> For thus says the Lord: David shall never lack (*yikkaret 'iš* [be cut out]) a man to sit on the throne of the house of Israel, and the Levitical priests shall never lack (*yikkaret 'iš* [be cut out]) a man in my presence to offer burnt offerings, to burn cereal offerings, and to make sacrifices for ever." (33:17-18)

> But to the house of the Rechabites Jeremiah said, "Thus says the Lord of hosts, the God of Israel: Because you have obeyed the command of Jonadab your father, and kept all his precepts, and done all that he commanded you, therefore thus says the Lord of hosts, the God of Israel: Jonadab the son of Rechab shall never lack (*yikkaret 'iš* [be cut out]) a man to stand before me." (35:18-19)[8]

Scripture, not Kingship and Temple, is the Legacy for the Future

Just as chapters 7 and 26 administered the final blow to the temple, chapter 36 functions as the coup de grâce for kingship. Zedekiah (the Lord is my righteousness) did not live up to his calling and proved unrighteous. Instead of raising up the crown of kingship in Jehoiakim (whose name means "the Lord will raise"), the Lord will bring it down in an action that will be immortalized in the scriptural scroll of Jeremiah: "Then Jeremiah took another scroll and gave it to Baruch the scribe, the son of Neriah, who wrote on it at the dictation of Jeremiah all the words of the scroll which Jehoiakim king of Judah had burned in the fire; and many similar words were added to them." (36:32)

---

[8] These are the only instances of the phrase *yikkaret 'iš* in Jeremiah.

The instruction (*musar*) that was despised, shredded, and burned by the leaders of Jerusalem will be preserved *as scripture* among people who "live in tents" and will be kept in the mobile "tent of meeting." The stone temple, into which that mobile tent was forced, will be brought down by God whose "cloudy" presence does not need a building. From that "tent" he will address his people out of the cloud with his instruction (*musar*) preserved on tablets and subsequently on scrolls. An overview of scripture will reveal that the temple that hosted the tent of meeting for a while was unnecessary for God (Is 66:1-2a). It was constructed not by the hand of God, but by the hand of man through a king willed by the people. Thus God's "cloudy" presence could leave it at will (Ezek 10) or could reside in it at will as well (1 Kg 8:10-11). His main residence, however, is in the text of the Law preserved in the ark of the testimony hosted in the tent of meeting:

> It shall be a continual burnt offering throughout your generations at the door of the tent of meeting before the Lord, where I will meet with you, to speak there to you. There I will meet with the people of Israel, and it shall be sanctified by my glory. (Ex 29:42-43)

> ... and you shall beat some of it very small, and put part of it before the testimony in the tent of meeting where I shall meet with you; it shall be for you most holy. (Ex 30:36)

> Now Moses used to take the tent and pitch it outside the camp, far off from the camp; and he called it the tent of meeting. And every one who sought the Lord would go out to the tent of meeting, which was outside the camp. Whenever Moses went out to the tent, all the people rose up, and every man stood at his tent door, and looked after Moses, until he had gone into the tent. When Moses entered the tent, the pillar of cloud would descend and stand at the door of the tent, and the Lord

would speak with Moses. And when all the people saw the pillar of cloud standing at the door of the tent, all the people would rise up and worship, every man at his tent door. Thus the Lord used to speak to Moses face to face, as a man speaks to his friend. When Moses turned again into the camp, his servant Joshua the son of Nun, a young man, did not depart from the tent. (Ex 33:7-11)

Then the cloud covered the tent of meeting, and the glory of the Lord filled the tabernacle. And Moses was not able to enter the tent of meeting, because the cloud abode upon it, and the glory of the Lord filled the tabernacle. Throughout all their journeys, whenever the cloud was taken up from over the tabernacle, the people of Israel would go onward; but if the cloud was not taken up, then they did not go onward till the day that it was taken up. For throughout all their journeys the cloud of the Lord was upon the tabernacle by day, and fire was in it by night, in the sight of all the house of Israel. (Ex 40:34-38)

The Lord called Moses, and spoke to him from the tent of meeting, saying… (Lev 1:1)

The Lord spoke to Moses in the wilderness of Sinai, in the tent of meeting, on the first day of the second month, in the second year after they had come out of the land of Egypt, saying… (Num 1:1)

And the Lord said to Moses, "Behold, the days approach when you must die; call Joshua, and present yourselves in the tent of meeting, that I may commission him." And Moses and Joshua went and presented themselves in the tent of meeting. And the Lord appeared in the tent in a pillar of cloud; and the pillar of cloud stood by the door of the tent. (Deut 31:14-15)

Then the whole congregation of the people of Israel assembled at Shiloh, and set up the tent of meeting there; the land lay subdued before them … These are the inheritances which Eleazar the priest and Joshua the son of Nun and the heads of the fathers' houses of

The Demise of the City and the Rise of Scripture

> the tribes of the people of Israel distributed by lot at Shiloh before the Lord, at the door of the tent of meeting. So they finished dividing the land. (Josh 18:1; 19:51)

> Then Solomon assembled the elders of Israel and all the heads of the tribes, the leaders of the fathers' houses of the people of Israel, before King Solomon in Jerusalem, to bring up the ark of the covenant of the Lord out of the city of David, which is Zion. And all the men of Israel assembled to King Solomon at the feast in the month Ethanim, which is the seventh month. And all the elders of Israel came, and the priests took up the ark. And they brought up the ark of the Lord, the tent of meeting, and all the holy vessels that were in the tent; the priests and the Levites brought them up ... *There was nothing in the ark except the two tables of stone which Moses put there at Horeb*, where the Lord made a covenant with the people of Israel, when they came out of the land of Egypt. And when the priests came out of the holy place, a cloud filled the house of the Lord, so that the priests could not stand to minister because of the cloud; for the glory of the Lord filled the house of the Lord. (1 Kg 8:1-4, 9-11)

God can reside where he pleases. In the time of Zedekiah and Jehoiakim he decided to reside in Jeremiah, his "fortified city," "against the whole land, against the kings of Judah, its princes, its priests, and the people of the land" (Jer 1:18). Through the lips of his new residence he emitted his testimony *at will*, just as he did through Moses:

> And you shall put into the ark the testimony which I shall give you ... And you shall put the mercy seat on the top of the ark; and in the ark you shall put the testimony that I shall give you. There I will meet with you, and from above the mercy seat, from between the two cherubim that are upon the ark of the testimony, I will speak with you of all that I will give you in commandment for the people of Israel. (Ex 25:16, 21-22)

The people disregarded the content of that testimony (32:7-10) and the tables containing that testimony, that is, "the work of God, and the writing was the writing of God, graven upon the tables" (v.16), were broken by Moses (v.19). Nevertheless, the Lord instructed Moses to re-write that testimony (34:27-29). Not only that, but the final scroll of Exodus contained the story of Israel's rebellion. Here also, when the original scroll containing "the words of the Lord" (Jer 36:2) was shredded and thrown into the fire by Jehoiakim (v.23), Jeremiah was summoned by God to have Baruch re-write those same words (vv.27-31), however, the updated scroll contained the king's misguided action. It is precisely this updated scroll, containing "the words of the Lord," that is the Book of Jeremiah, that became as much scripture as the Book of Exodus.

Included here for perusal by my readers is the entirety of Jeremiah 36 with annotations so that they may see and hear the impressive original and realize for themselves how the "voice" (*qol*) which utters God's "words" (*debarim*)—and not a supposedly ethereal eternal "word" *à la* Plato, as advocated by classical theology—becomes scripture:

> ¹In the fourth year of Jehoiakim the son of Josiah, king of Judah, this word came to Jeremiah from the Lord: ²"*Take a scroll* and write on it all the words (*debarim*) that I have spoken (*dibbarti*) to you against Israel and Judah and all the nations, from the day I spoke to you, *from the days of Josiah until today*. ³It may be that the house of Judah will hear all the evil which I intend to do to them, so that every one may turn from his evil way, and that I may forgive their iniquity and their sin." ⁴Then Jeremiah called Baruch the son of Neriah, and Baruch wrote upon a scroll at the dictation (*mippi*; from [out of] the mouth) of Jeremiah all the words of the Lord which he had spoken to him. ⁵And Jeremiah ordered Baruch, saying, "I am debarred from going to the house of the Lord; ⁶so

you are to go, and on a fast day in the hearing of all the people in the Lord's house you shall read (*qara'ta*; from the verb *qara*'⁹ [read aloud] for others to hear) the words of the Lord from the scroll which you have written at my dictation (*mippi*; from [out of] my mouth). You shall read them also *in the hearing of* all the men of Judah who come out of their cities. ⁷It may be that their supplication will come before the Lord, and that every one will turn from his evil way, for great is the anger and wrath that the Lord has pronounced against this people." ⁸And Baruch the son of Neriah did all that Jeremiah the prophet ordered him about reading from the scroll the words of the Lord in the Lord's house. ⁹In the fifth year of Jehoiakim the son of Josiah, king of Judah, in the ninth month, all the people in Jerusalem and all the people who came from the cities of Judah to Jerusalem proclaimed a fast before the Lord. ¹⁰Then, in the hearing of all the people, Baruch *read* the words of Jeremiah *from the scroll*, in the house of the Lord, in the chamber of Gemariah the son of Shaphan the secretary, which was in the upper court, at the entry of the New Gate of the Lord's house. ¹¹When Micaiah the son of Gemariah, son of Shaphan, *heard* all the words of the Lord *from the scroll*, ¹²he went down to the king's house, into the secretary's chamber; and all the princes were sitting there: Elishama the secretary, Delaiah the son of Shemaiah, Elnathan the son of Achbor, Gemariah the son of Shaphan, Zedekiah the son of Hananiah, and all the princes. ¹³And Micaiah told them *all the words that he had heard*, when Baruch *read* the scroll *in the hearing of* the people. ¹⁴Then all the princes sent Jehudi the son of Nethaniah, son of Shelemiah, son of Cushi, to say to Baruch, "Take in your hand the scroll that you read in the hearing of the people, and come." So Baruch the son of Neriah took the scroll in his hand and came to them. ¹⁵And they said to him, "Sit down and read it." So Baruch read it to them. ¹⁶When they heard all the words, they turned one to another in fear; and they said to Baruch, "We must report all these

---

⁹ Whence *qur'an*, Islam's scripture, that is to be "read aloud" for the people to "hear."

words to the king." ¹⁷Then they asked Baruch, "Tell us, how did you write all these words? Was it at his dictation (*mippiw*; from [out of] his mouth)?" ¹⁸Baruch answered them, "He dictated (*yiqra'*; from the verb *qara'*¹⁰ [enunciate aloud]) all these words to me, while I wrote them with ink on the scroll." ¹⁹Then the princes said to Baruch, "Go and hide, you and Jeremiah, and let no one know where you are." ²⁰So they went into the court to the king, having put the scroll in the chamber of Elishama the secretary; and they reported all the words to the king. ²¹Then the king sent Jehudi to get the scroll, and he took it from the chamber of Elishama the secretary; and Jehudi *read it* to the king and all the princes who stood beside the king. ²²It was the ninth month, and the king was sitting in the winter house and there was a fire burning in the brazier before him. ²³As Jehudi read three or four columns, the king would cut them off with a penknife and throw them into the fire in the brazier, until the entire scroll was consumed in the fire that was in the brazier. ²⁴Yet neither the king, nor any of his servants who heard all these words, was afraid, nor did they rend their garments. ²⁵Even when Elnathan and Delaiah and Gemariah urged the king not to burn the scroll, he would not listen to them. ²⁶And the king commanded Jerahmeel the king's son and Seraiah the son of Azri-el and Shelemiah the son of Abdeel to seize Baruch the secretary and Jeremiah the prophet, but the Lord hid them. ²⁷Now, after the king had burned the scroll with the words which Baruch wrote at Jeremiah's dictation (*mippi*; from [out of] the mouth), the word of the Lord came to Jeremiah: ²⁸"*Take another scroll* and write on it all the former words that were in the first scroll, which Jehoiakim the king of Judah has burned. ²⁹And concerning Jehoiakim king of Judah you shall say, 'Thus says the Lord, You have burned this scroll, saying, "Why have you written in it that the king of Babylon will certainly come and destroy this land, and will cut off from it man and beast?" ³⁰Therefore thus says the Lord concerning Jehoiakim king

---

¹⁰ See previous fn.

of Judah, *He shall have none to sit upon the throne of David, and his dead body shall be cast out to the heat by day and the frost by night.* ³¹And I will punish him and his offspring and his servants for their iniquity; I will bring upon them, and upon the inhabitants of Jerusalem, and upon the men of Judah, all the evil that I have pronounced against them, but they would not hear.'" ³²Then Jeremiah *took another scroll* and gave it to Baruch the scribe, the son of Neriah, who wrote on it at the dictation (*mippi*; from [out of] the mouth) of Jeremiah all the words of the scroll which Jehoiakim king of Judah had burned in the fire; *and many similar words were added to them.*

Chapter 10
Message over Messenger

Return to Egypt

The function of chapters 37-45 parallels that of Deuteronomy: the messenger's imperfect behavior does not blemish the divine message that stands on its own. It is the book that will guide the yet unborn generations on the right path. Though Moses was barred entry into the earth of promise, his law insured that Joshua would secure the inheritances for the tribes. Here also, although Jeremiah will end up in Egypt, against the command of God, the words uttered by the prophet's lips will remain valid for "the remnant of Judah."[1] In fact these words will be valid even for an Ethiopian outsider (39:15-18).[2]

The stories of Ebed-melech, the Ethiopian eunuch, and Zedekiah, King of Judah, contrast their strikingly divergent attitudes. While Zedekiah was continually tergiversating in his attitude (37:3-21; 38:14-23), even asking Jeremiah to cover up for him (vv.24-27), Ebed-melech took a steadfast stand for the prophet:

> [1]Now Shephatiah the son of Mattan, Gedaliah the son of Pashhur, and Jucal the son of Shelemiah, and Pashhur the son of Malchiah heard the words that Jeremiah was saying to all the people, [2]"Thus says the Lord, He who stays in this city shall die by the sword, by famine, and by pestilence; but he who goes out to the Chaldeans shall live; he shall have his life as a prize of war, and live. [3]Thus

---

[1] Jer 40:11, 15; 42:15, 19; 43:5; 44:12, 14, 28.
[2] The story of the Ethiopian eunuch and the scroll of Isaiah in Acts 8:26-40 is built on this premise.

says the Lord, This city shall surely be given into the hand of the army of the king of Babylon and be taken." ⁴Then the princes said to the king, "Let this man be put to death, for he is weakening the hands of the soldiers who are left in this city, and the hands of all the people, by speaking such words to them. For this man is not seeking the welfare of this people, but their harm." ⁵King Zedekiah said, "Behold he is in your hands, for the king can do nothing against you." ⁶So they took Jeremiah and cast him into the cistern of Malchiah, the king's son, which was in the court of the guard, letting Jeremiah down by ropes. And there was no water in the cistern, but only mire, and Jeremiah sank in the mire. ⁷When Ebed-melech the Ethiopian, a eunuch, who was in the king's house, heard that they had put Jeremiah into the cistern— the king was sitting in the Benjamin Gate—⁸Ebed-melech went from the king's house and said to the king, ⁹"My lord the King, these men have done evil in all that they did to Jeremiah the prophet by casting him into the cistern; and he will die there of hunger, for there is no bread left in the city." ¹⁰Then the king commanded Ebed-melech, the Ethiopian, "Take three men with you from here, and lift Jeremiah the prophet out of the cistern before he dies." ¹¹So Ebed-melech took the men with him and went to the house of the king, to a wardrobe of the storehouse, and took from there old rags and worn-out clothes, which he let down to Jeremiah in the cistern by ropes. ¹²Then Ebed-melech the Ethiopian said to Jeremiah, "Put the rags and clothes between your armpits and the ropes." Jeremiah did so. ¹³Then they drew Jeremiah up with ropes and lifted him out of the cistern. And Jeremiah remained in the court of the guard. (38:1-13)

Whereas Zedekiah proved unworthy of his name, the eunuch acted worthily of his name, thus putting Zedekiah to shame. Since the name Ebed-melech (*'ebed melek*) means "servant of [God] the King," the Ethiopian actually behaved as a true king, the consummate "servant of the Lord," would have. The moral of this story parallels that of Jonadab son of Rechab: two totally common outsiders prove to be more "kingly" than the king of Judah. That is why, on the one hand, Zedekiah suffered the most abject of sentences:

> When Jerusalem was taken, all the princes of the king of Babylon came and sat in the middle gate: Nergal-sharezer, Samgar-nebo, Sarsechim the Rabsaris, Nergal-sharezer the Rabmag, with all the rest of the officers of the king of Babylon. When Zedekiah king of Judah and all the soldiers saw them, they fled, going out of the city at night by way of the king's garden through the gate between the two walls; and they went toward the Arabah. But the army of the Chaldeans pursued them, and overtook Zedekiah in the plains of Jericho; and when they had taken him, they brought him up to Nebuchadrezzar king of Babylon, at Riblah, in the land of Hamath; and he passed sentence upon him. The king of Babylon slew the sons of Zedekiah at Riblah before his eyes; and the king of Babylon slew all the nobles of Judah. He put out the eyes of Zedekiah, and bound him in fetters to take him to Babylon. (39:3-7)

On the other hand, Ebed-melech was treated on par with Jeremiah in that the Lord promises in a direct address to him (vv.15-16) to "deliver (*hiṣṣil*) you on that day, says the Lord, and you shall not be given into the hand of the men of whom you are afraid" (v.17) just as he promised Jeremiah: "Do not be dismayed by them, lest I dismay you before them ... They will fight against you; but they shall not prevail against you, for I am with you, says the Lord, to deliver (*hiṣṣil*) you." (1:17b, 19)

Furthermore, Ebed-melech's attitude proves to be an indictment on "the remnant of Judah" even after the demise of Zedekiah. Despite the objections of Jeremiah (37:6-10), Zedekiah appealed to Egypt for help against the Babylonians, an action that proved ill-fated (39:1-10). In yet another anti-

Babylonian move Ishmael, the son of Nethaniah, assassinated Gedaliah (41:1-3), the governor of Judah appointed by Nebuchadrezzar (40:7). Ishmael went on a rampage killing many people (41:9). He then decided to flee to Ammon (vv.10, 15) with those whom he spared (v.8, 10) in order to avoid reprisal by the Babylonians for having killed Gedaliah (v.18). Even Johanan the son of Kareah, who tried to stand against Ishmael in order to prevent further carnage (vv.11-14), decided to go to Egypt with his followers (vv.16-17) to escape reprisal from the Babylonians (v.18). Since Jeremiah had expressed his dissatisfaction with Zedekiah's appeal to Egypt, Johanan thought it safer to consult with the prophet concerning God's will and promised to abide by it, whatever it might be (42:1-6). As expected, Jeremiah's response was that Johanan's party should desist from going to Egypt and stay in Judah (vv.7-12). God's verdict of punishment would not spare "the remnant of Judah" even in Egypt itself (vv.13-22). Not only did Johanan renege on his promise (43:1-3), but he and his followers forced Jeremiah and Baruch to go with them (vv.4-7). This action unleashed the Lord's ire against the Judahites in Egypt at the hand, no less, of his "servant" Nebuchadrezzar (vv.8-13).

The Queen of Heaven

Chapter 44 confirms that God's decision to punish the Judahites in Egypt was justified as well as just. It rejoins Ezekiel's teaching that the forefathers committed idolatry while they were still in Egypt:

> Will you judge them [the elders of Israel], son of man, will you judge them? Then let them know the abominations of their fathers, and say to them, Thus says the Lord God: On the day when I chose Israel, I swore to the seed of the house of Jacob, making myself known to them in the land of Egypt, I swore to

> them, saying, I am the Lord your God. On that day I swore to them that I would bring them out of the land of Egypt into a land that I had searched out for them, a land flowing with milk and honey, the most glorious of all lands. And I said to them, Cast away the detestable things your eyes feast on, every one of you, and do not defile yourselves with the idols of Egypt; I am the Lord your God. But they rebelled against me and would not listen to me; they did not every man cast away the detestable things their eyes feasted on, nor did they forsake the idols of Egypt. (Ezek 20:4-8)

Here, in Jeremiah, we hear that their progeny, the Judahites, did the same thing; they persisted in their idolatry after having been warned not to do so. Just as their forebears worshipped the idols of Egypt, the Judahites made offerings to "the queen of heaven" (Jer 7:18; 44:17-18, 25). The scriptural tradition that the people who were graced with the divine law continually persisted in their disobedience to the commandments of that law is at its clearest in the introduction to Psalm 78:

> He established a testimony in Jacob, and appointed a law in Israel, which he commanded our fathers to teach to their children; that the next generation might know them, the children yet unborn, and arise and tell them to their children, so that they should set their hope in God, and not forget the works of God, but keep his commandments; and that they should not be like their fathers, a stubborn and rebellious generation, a generation whose heart was not steadfast, whose spirit was not faithful to God. (vv.5-8)

The same tradition finds its most incisive expression on the lips of God himself who traces it back to Abraham while stressing that disobedience to the Lord continued uninterrupted up till Joshua's time:

> Then Joshua gathered all the tribes of Israel to Shechem, and summoned the elders, the heads, the judges, and the officers of Israel; and they presented themselves before God. And Joshua said to all the people, "Thus says the Lord, the God of Israel, 'Your fathers lived of old beyond the Euphrates, Terah, the father of Abraham and of Nahor; and they served other gods. Then I took your father Abraham from beyond the River and led him through all the land of Canaan, and made his offspring many' ... Now therefore fear the Lord, and serve him in sincerity and in faithfulness; put away the gods which your fathers served beyond the River, and in Egypt, and serve the Lord." (Josh 24:1-3, 14)

Another traditional scriptural feature found in Jeremiah 44 is that the kings of Judah and Israel are no better than the kings of the nations. The institution of kingship—the common expression of human authority over other humans—is tantamount to idolatry toward the sole valid King, the Lord himself:

> Then all the elders of Israel gathered together and came to Samuel at Ramah, and said to him, "Behold, you are old and your sons do not walk in your ways; now appoint for us *a king to govern us like all the nations.*" But the thing displeased Samuel when they said, "Give us a king to govern us." And Samuel prayed to the Lord. And the Lord said to Samuel, "Hearken to the voice of the people in all that they say to you; for they have not rejected you, but they have rejected me from being king over them. According to all the deeds which they have done to me, from the day I brought them up out of Egypt even to this day, forsaking me and serving other gods, so they are also doing to you. Now then, hearken to their voice; only, you shall solemnly warn them, and show them the ways of the king who shall reign over them." (1 Sam 8:4-9)

Message over Messenger

That the author of Jeremiah had this passage in mind can be seen in his multiple references to Mizpah (40:6, 8, 10, 12, 13, 15; 41:1, 3, 6, 10, 14, 16) as the place of the Judahites' rebellion against Nebuchadrezzar whom God appointed to carry out his will. Mizpah is precisely the locality where the people officially requested that Samuel appoint a king over them (1 Sam 10:17-24). That is why, upon his decision to free the Judahites from the Babylonian captivity, the Lord ends his harangue of the consistent sins of idolatry by Israel with the following statement:

> What is in your mind shall never happen—the thought, "Let us be like the nations, like the tribes of the countries, and worship wood and stone." As I live, says the Lord God, surely with a mighty hand and an outstretched arm, and with wrath poured out, *I will be king over you.* (Ezek 20:32-33)

This explains why the last words of Jeremiah to the Judahites in Egypt put Pharaoh on equal footing with Zedekiah:

> This shall be the sign to you, says the Lord, that I will punish you in this place, in order that you may know that my words will surely stand against you for evil: Thus says the Lord, Behold, I will give Pharaoh Hophra king of Egypt into the hand of his enemies and into the hand of those who seek his life, as I gave Zedekiah king of Judah into the hand of Nebuchadrezzar king of Babylon, who was his enemy and sought his life. (Jer 44:29-30)

The Book of Jeremiah canonizes itself as scripture

At the conclusion of the section (ch.45), before the oracles concerning the nations (chs.46-51), we have a direct reference to the "book" of chapter 36:

> In the fourth year of Jehoiakim the son of Josiah, king of Judah, this word came to Jeremiah from the Lord: "Take a scroll and write on it all the words that I have spoken to you against Israel

and Judah and all the nations, from the day I spoke to you, from the days of Josiah until today. It may be that the house of Judah will hear all the evil which I intend to do to them, so that every one may turn from his evil way, and that I may forgive their iniquity and their sin." (36:1-3)

> The word that Jeremiah the prophet spoke to Baruch the son of Neriah, when he wrote these words in a book at the dictation of Jeremiah, in the fourth year of Jehoiakim the son of Josiah, king of Judah. (45:1)

However, just as the original book was updated after its burning by Jehoiakim (36:32), here also we hear that the previous updated version is revised with the addition of chapters 37-44. This process, already announced in 36:2 (Take a scroll and write on it all the words that I have spoken to you against Israel and Judah *and all the nations*) is also referenced in 45:4 (Behold, what I have built I am breaking down, and what I have planted I am plucking up—that is, the whole land ['*ereṣ*; earth]) and will later include the oracles regarding the nations (chs.45-51), as we shall hear at the end of the Book of Jeremiah:

> The word which Jeremiah the prophet commanded Seraiah the son of Neriah, son of Mahseiah, when he went with Zedekiah king of Judah to Babylon, in the fourth year of his reign. Seraiah was the quartermaster. Jeremiah wrote in a book all the evil that should come upon Babylon, all these words that are written concerning Babylon. And Jeremiah said to Seraiah: "When you come to Babylon, see that you read all these words, and say, 'O Lord, thou hast said concerning this place that thou wilt cut it off, so that nothing shall dwell in it, neither man nor beast, and it shall be desolate for ever.' When you finish reading this book, bind a stone to it, and cast it into the midst of the Euphrates, and say, 'Thus shall Babylon sink, to rise no more, because of the evil that I

am bringing upon her.'" Thus far are the words of Jeremiah. (51:59-64)

Notice how "the words of Jeremiah" at the end of v.64 bracket the entire book which starts with the same phrase "The words of Jeremiah" (1:1). It occurs only once more in 36:10 where it refers to the words that constitute the content of the scroll presented to Jehoiakim. Such cannot be happenstance; rather it reflects intentionality on the author's part. This is borne out by the use of another word in the Book of Jeremiah. Besides 51:59, the name of Baruch's "grandfather" Mahseiah (*maḥseyah* [the Lord is refuge] from the root *ḥasah*) occurs only once more in the Book of Consolation (chs.30-33): "I gave the deed of purchase to Baruch the son of Neriah son of Mahseiah in the presence of Hanamel my cousin, in the presence of the witnesses who signed the deed of purchase, and in the presence of all the Jews who were sitting in the court of the guard." (32:12) The only other instance of the root *ḥasah* in Jeremiah appears as the noun *maḥseh* in 17:17 (Be not a terror to me; thou art my refuge [*maḥseh*] in the day of evil), which is part of the chapters (1-25) designated as "this book" (25:13a).[3]

Thus the Book of Jeremiah is not only a unitary production, it is also intentionally canonizing itself, that is, "the words of Jeremiah" are nothing else save "the words of the Lord" valid for all "nations and kingdoms" (1:9-10). With this mind, the venerable tradition that a community of believers, through the medium of authoritative synods and councils, can decide for the canonical value of the scriptural books is invalid. In scripture the adage *vox populi vox dei* never holds water. It is always the "voice

---

[3] See my comments earlier.

of God" *as inscribed in and heard out of the actual words of scripture* that presents itself as valid in and of itself.[4]

---

[4] Paul, the Apostle to the nations, correctly understood this; his writings repeatedly resound with the phrase "as it is written."

Chapter 11
Oracles concerning the Nations

As is characteristic in scripture, Judah and Israel have the lion's share of divine prosecution because they were privy to God's law granted to their forebears. Their indictment was covered in chapters 26-44. Now that he has addressed Judah and Israel, Jeremiah turns his attention to the other nations.

At the conclusion of the first "book" (Jer 25:13a), Jeremiah communicated God's message "against *all* the nations" (25:13b). After mention of Jerusalem and Judah (v.18), he listed the other nations (vv.19-26). Egypt headed the list (25:19). The priority is given to Egypt because, against God's instruction, Judah sought its help to fend off the Babylonians. To remind the hearers that God's scale of justice is the same for all, Egypt is addressed here (46:2-28) in terms similar to those used toward Judah.

First and foremost, "Go up to Gilead, and take balm, O virgin daughter of Egypt! in vain you have used many medicines; there is no healing for you" (46:11) fully corresponds to "You shall say to them this word: 'Let my eyes run down with tears night and day, and let them not cease, for the virgin daughter of my people is smitten with a great wound, with a very grievous blow'" (14:17). See also "The virgin Israel has done a very horrible thing" (18:13b); "Again I will build you, and you shall be built, O virgin Israel!" (31:4a); and "Return, O virgin Israel, return to these your cities" (v.21). Secondly, Egypt is punished at Nebuchadrezzar's hand (46:13) in the same vein as Judah (44:30). Thirdly, in both cases, the kings are specifically targeted (46:17 and 44:30) because the Lord is the only King: "Call the name of Pharaoh, king of Egypt, 'Noisy one who lets the hour go by.' As I live, says the King, whose name is the Lord of hosts, like Tabor among the mountains, and like Carmel by the sea, shall one come." (46:17-18) Lastly, and no less importantly, just as Judah will be restored, so shall Egypt be restored.[1] And, as if to remind Judah not to boast, the oracle against Egypt ends with the following caveat: "Fear not, O Jacob my servant, says the Lord, for I am with you. I will make a full end of all the nations to which I have driven you, but of you I will not make a full end. *I will chasten you in just measure, and I will by no means leave you unpunished.*" (46:28)

The divine indictment then covers those nations surrounding Judah—Philistia (ch.47), Moab (ch.48), Ammon (49:1-6), Edom (vv.7-22), Damascus (vv.23-27), and the kingdoms of Arabia (vv.28-33; see 25:23-24).[2] Even Ishmael's small contingent of eight men that fled to the Ammonites (41:15), and all such contingents that may have sought refuge in neighboring areas, will not escape the all-seeing eye of the Lord. They will not fare better than the followers of Johanan who ended up in Egypt (ch.42-43).

Before handling Babylon we unexpectedly hear of the fate of Elam (49:34-39), the power that would eventually bring down Babylon (Is 21:1-10). The reason for this is twofold. On the one hand, it establishes that God's hegemony extends well beyond the immediate horizon of Jerusalem and that his reach extends into the unseen future. On the other hand and as a corollary, the hearers, who are about to listen in detail to the fate of Babylon (chs.50-51), will more readily accept the oracle against that city in spite of evidence to the contrary that is surrounding them.

---

[1] This topic is also found in Ezekiel (29:13-14).
[2] Compare with Am 1:3-2:3.

Oracles concerning the Nations

Still, just as in the case of Egypt, and in order to take away from the Judahites any ground for boastfulness or derision, at the end of chapter 49 one hears that Elam will be restored by the Lord himself: "But in the latter days I will restore the fortunes of Elam, says the Lord." (v.39)

The indictment against Babylon (chs. 50 and 51) is magisterially constructed in that it brings together signature elements from both Isaiah and Ezekiel as well as those in Jeremiah itself. The result is that the ending of Jeremiah functions as the "center" of scripture. This corroborates what was discussed earlier regarding *musar*,[3] and that the Book of Jeremiah "pulls together" the entire Old Testament scripture. What sets the tone is a clear reference to the "new covenant" in the Book of Consolation and to the precedence of Israel over Judah in that promise:

> Behold, the days are coming, says the Lord, when I will make a new covenant with the house of Israel and the house of Judah, not like the covenant which I made with their fathers when I took them by the hand to bring them out of the land of Egypt, my covenant which they broke, though I was their husband, says the Lord. But this is the covenant which I will make with the house of Israel after those days, says the Lord: I will put my law within them, and I will write it upon their hearts; and I will be their God, and they shall be my people. (Jer 31:31-33)

> In those days and in that time, says the Lord, the people of Israel and the people of Judah shall come together, weeping as they come; and they shall seek the Lord their God. They shall ask the way to Zion, with faces turned toward it, saying, "Come, let us join ourselves to the Lord in an everlasting covenant which will never be forgotten." (50:4-5)

---

[3] See pp. 63-71.

The pasture (*naweh*; sheepfold; often translated as "habitation" in RSV) that spans chapter 50 (vv.7, 19, 44) is a classic noun that also appears in Isaiah and Ezekiel and throughout Jeremiah (9:9 [Hebrew]; 10:25: 23:3, 10; 25:30, 37; 31:23; 33:12; 49:19, 20). "Holy One of Israel" (50:29) and "redeemer" (*go'el*; v.34) are staples of the Book of Isaiah. What is interesting is that the noun *go'el* is qualified as *ḥazaq* (strong), which is one of the two constituent roots of the name *yeḥezqe'l* (Ezekiel) whose meaning is "God has proved [shown] himself as (the) strong(est)."[4] Such a choice at the end of the book may well be a deft allusion to both Isaiah and Ezekiel, which would fit the role of Jeremiah being the scriptural "center." Finally, and again in order not to allow the Judahite hearers to boast or gloat, the author makes sure to drill into their ears that Babylon will fall due to its sin of idolatry (Jer 50:2, 38; 51:17, 47, 52), just as was the case with Judah (8:19; 10:5, 8, 14; 16:18).

The concluding chapter 52 is a carbon copy of 2 Kings 24:8-25:30. Its function is to remind the hearers that the new covenant inscribed, that is, scripturalized in the Book of Jeremiah and the promised salvation lie forever ahead. Put otherwise, the hearer of the book, whether the original addressee or anyone in a subsequent generation, is always put in the position of looking forward to and thus waiting for their realization in the future. The Lord remains always "coming" and is never already here. Hence the "literal" validity of scripture stands for every generation. Willy-nilly, the hearers of Jeremiah 52 are catapulted back to the last book of the Prior Prophets and are forced to hear again and again the messages of hope of Isaiah and Jeremiah. And lest those hearers who proceed beyond Jeremiah into the last two scrolls of the Latter Prophets, Ezekiel

---

[4] See also earlier "For the Lord has ransomed Jacob, and has redeemed (*ga'al*) him from hands too strong (*ḥazaq*) for him." (Jer 31:11)

and the Twelve, be lured into thinking otherwise, the last chapter of the Scroll of the Twelve catapults them even further back in the Prior Prophets where they encounter "Elijah the prophet," and even beyond that to the Law of the Lord's servant Moses. Thus the hearers are forced to listen again and again to scripture that gives them hope that the Lord is indeed "coming":

> For behold, the day comes, burning like an oven, when all the arrogant and all evildoers will be stubble; the day that comes shall burn them up, says the Lord of hosts, so that it will leave them neither root nor branch. But for you who fear my name the sun of righteousness shall rise, with healing in its wings. You shall go forth leaping like calves from the stall. And you shall tread down the wicked, for they will be ashes under the soles of your feet, on the day when I act, says the Lord of hosts. Remember the law of my servant Moses, the statutes and ordinances that I commanded him at Horeb for all Israel. Behold, I will send you Elijah the prophet before the great and terrible day of the Lord comes. And he will turn the hearts of fathers to their children and the hearts of children to their fathers, lest I come and smite the land with a curse. (Mal 4:1-5)

Put succinctly, scripture is tantamount to the Lord's "coming" to judge and hopefully to vindicate every generation of hearers. There is nothing "beyond" or "after" scripture as is falsely taught in both Judaism and Christianity that tend to glorify the post-scriptural "traditions of men." Nor is one to extrapolate on it as is done in classical Jewish and Christian theology. As Chrysostom remarked already in the fourth century, "scripture is its own interpreter"; nothing precedes it or extends it. It is its own world and challenges us to enter it and be engulfed in it, should we decide to accept *its* message of salvation.

Further Reading

Commentaries and Studies

Bou Raad J., O.A.M. *Malheur annoncé, Malheur dénoncé. Étude rhétorique de Jérémie 6*. Baabda, Lebanon: Editions de l'Université Antonine, 2008.

Dearman, J. A. *Jeremiah/Lamentations*. NIV Application Commentary. Grand Rapids, MI: Zondervan, 2002.

Dempsey, C. J. *Jeremiah. Preacher of Grace, Poet of Truth*. Interfaces. Collegeville, MN: Liturgical Press, 2007.

Joo, S. *Provocation and Punishment: The Anger of God in the Book of Jeremiah and Deuteronomistic Theology*. Berlin/New York: de Gruyter, 2006.

Kalmanofsky, A. *Terror All Around: The Rhetoric of Horror in the Book of Jeremiah*. London/New York: T & T Clark, 2008.

Kessler, M. (ed.) *Reading the Book of Jeremiah. A Search for Coherence*. Winona Lake, IN: Eisenbrauns, 2004.

Longman III, T. *Jeremiah, Lamentations*. NICOT. Peabody, MA: Hendrickson, 2008.

Stulman, L. *Jeremiah*. Abingdon Old Testament Commentaries. Nashville: Abingdon, 2005.

Articles

Aejmelaeus, A. "Jeremiah at the turning point of history: the function of Jer. xxv 1-14 in the Book of Jeremiah." *Vetus Testamentum* 52 (2002) 459-82.

Avioz, M. "The call for revenge in Jeremiah's complaints (Jer xi-xx)." *Vetus Testamentum* 55 (2005) 429-38.

Bungishabaku, K. "La connaissance de YHWH selon Jérémie: Une étude intra-intertextuelle." *Old Testament Essays* 21 (2008) 38-60.

Gosse, B. "La nouvelle alliance de Jérémie 31,31-34: Du livre d'Ezéchiel au livre de Jérémie." *Zeitschrift für die alttestamentliche Wissenschaft* 116 (2004) 568-80.

Gosse, B. "Le prophète Jérémie en Jer 11,18-12,6 dans le cadre du livre de Jérémie et en rapport avec le Psautier." *Zeitschrift für die alttestamentliche Wissenschaft* 118 (2006) 549-57.

Hill, J. "The Book of Jeremiah MT and Early Second Temple Conflicts About Prophets and Prophecy." *Australian Biblical Review* 50 (2002) 28-42.

Hill, J. "Writing the Prophetic Word—The Production of the Book of Jeremiah." *Australian Biblical Review* 57 (2009) 22-33.

Holt E. K. "The Meaning of an *Inclusio:* A Theological Interpretation of the Book of Jeremiah MT." *Scandinavian Journal of the Old Testament* 17 (2003) 183-205.

Kalmanofsky, A. "The Dangerous Sisters of Jeremiah and Ezekiel." *Journal of Biblical Literature* 139 (2011) 299-312.

Kruger, P. A. "A Woman Will 'Encompass' a Man." *Biblica* 89 (2008) 380-88.

Martin, M. W. and Whitclark, J. A. "Le prophète Jérémie en Jer 11,18-12,6 dans le cadre du livre de Jérémie et en rapport avec le Psautier." *Zeitschrift für die alttestamentliche Wissenschaft* 118 (2006) 549-57.

Murphy, S. J. "The Quest for the Structure of the Book of Jeremiah." *Bibliotheca Sacra* 166 (2009) 306-18.

di Pede, E. "Jérémie et les rois de Juda, Sédécias et Joaqim." *Vetus Testamentum* 56 (2006) 452-69.

di Pede, E. "Un oracle pour les Récabites (Jr 35,18-19 TM) ou à leur propos (42,18-19 LXX)?" *Scandinavian Journal of the Old Testament* 20 (2006) 96-109.

di Pede, E. "Le refus et l'espoir: L'intrigue de Jr 32-45." *Ephemerides Theologicae Lovanienses* 80 (2004) 373-401.

Further Reading

di Pede, E. "Jérémie 'prophète' dans la LXX et dans le TM." *Estudios Biblicos* 67 (2009) 101-10.

di Pede, E. "Le récit de la prise de Jérusalem (Jer 46 LXX et 39 TM): son importance dans le récit et son impact sur le lecteur." *Biblische Zeitschrift* 52 (2008) 579-90.

Snyman, S. D. "(Dis-)unity in Jeremiah 20:7-13?" *Old Testament Essays* 12 (1999) 733-51.

Wessels, W. "Zion, beautiful city of God—Zion theology in the book of Jeremiah." *Verbum et Ecclesia* 27 (2007) 729-48.

Wessels, W. J. "Prophet Versus Prophet in the Book of Jeremiah: In Search of the True Prophets." *Old Testament Essays* 22 (2009) 733-51.

Wessels, W. J. "The Newness of the Word: Hermeneutical Implications of the Reinterpretation of Prophetic Words in the Book of Jeremiah." *Journal for Semitics* 19 (2010) 214-34.

Wessels, W. J. "True and False Prophets: Who Is To Decide? A Perspective from Jeremiah 23:9-40." *Journal for Semitics* 21 (2012) 137-56.

Yates, G. E. "Narrative Parallelism and the 'Jehoiakim Frame': A Reading Strategy for Jeremiah 26-45." *Journal of the Evangelical Theological Society* 48 (2005) 263-81.

Yates, G. "New Exodus and No Exodus in Jeremiah 26-45: Promise and Warning to the Exiles in Babylon." *Tyndale Bulletin* 57 (2006) 1-22.

www.ingramcontent.com/pod-product-compliance
Lightning Source LLC
Chambersburg PA
CBHW032118090426

42743CB00007B/391